AUTOBIOGRAPHY AND POLITICAL PERSPECTIVE OF POLITOLOGUE
VILIO BACETTE

The Haitian Community Without a Community Center

authorHOUSE®

AuthorHouse™
1663 Liberty Drive
Bloomington, IN 47403
www.authorhouse.com
Phone: 833-262-8899

Published by AuthorHouse 07/29/2024

ISBN: 978-1-6655-7189-0 (sc)
ISBN: 978-1-6655-7187-6 (hc)
ISBN: 978-1-6655-7188-3 (e)

Library of Congress Control Number: 2022917888

Print information available on the last page.

Any people depicted in stock imagery provided by Getty Images are models, and such images are being used for illustrative purposes only. Certain stock imagery © Getty Images.

This book is printed on acid-free paper.

CONTENTS

ABOUT THE AUTHOR

My Name is Vilio Bacette, and I am from Haiti in Port-AU-Prince, which is the capital, and Banlieue called Carrefour situated south of downtown. I was born in a family of four boys and two girls. We were raised very poorly. However, our unique chance was to continue our education. I have always believed my key to success is education. To repeat some scholars, "Knowledge is power."

I grew up in Carrefour and went to a public primary school called Damocles Vieux. Most parts in my secondary school were at Jean Jacques Rousseau a regular student and another part as an irregular student. I take advantage of that occasion to send a flow of gratitude to the students and professors in Damocles Vieux. I salute my comrade's students and professors of Jean Jacques Rousseau, a prestigious school. I was worried about people's living conditions at school, including mine. To wear clothes, to eat food were a phenomenon. People always kept their distance from me at first sight, but in a short time I got their appreciation. At first, they did not know my talent, ideology, and savoir-faire in that political sphere. To help people and myself, I engaged in politics.

My first empiric task was to hear people, accept their criticism, and understand their desires. The next step was to combine the different dichotomies and create an organization to address the commune demand, nothing but negative and positive rights. Some political friends and my brother decided to build up the public political movement called "Jeunes du pays en voie de développement (J.P.D.)." Translated meaning—Young people from developing countries. In 1989 a wind of change blew in Haiti and carried Jean Bertrand Aristide in power. Inaugurated on February 7, 1991, and overthrown in September 1991 by the army. It was reported a significant number of people died, and several thousand were injured. My family was saved, but I had to change my location because enemies came after me. Nonetheless, they came to shoot in the air to intimidate my family. In the next chapter, my family and I left Haiti on July 27, 1994. We entered Chicago on July 28, 1994.

Arrival at Chicago

My family is composed of my pregnant wife, Mimose Opont Bacette, and my two boys. Furthermore, I arrived in Chicago on July 28, 1994, around 11:30 a.m. at O'Hare airport. We were welcomed by Pastor Flecheimann of Lutheran church and his family, and Martine Theodore, the Director of the Haitian Americans center. While this may be true, I did not speak English, but I did not have relatives in America. The support given from the government had a duration of six months. Further, the government paid our rent and furnished us with some food stamps for the month, which we could not pay the bill. That forced me to get a job quickly to feed my family and help my relatives in Haiti.

The Education

The week after, an African American lady, named Lourdes, who spoke French sent me to the office for refugees. It was located at Sheridan Road. I was also sent to Truman College to study English. At the same time, I learned English and American customs, explored the area, and looked for a job to establish my family. Furthermore, after some classes, I went to Devry to learn electronics. I transferred my credits to Northeastern Illinois University to enroll in political science for one or two semesters. In comparison, my first professor told the class that the bachelor program took four years to graduate, which was not my original plan.

Equally important, I had my hands full, working a full-time job, monitoring my children's school activities, and being involved in community activities, whose goal was to build a representative Haitian American Community Center.

Analogous to that, I continued the program. Finally, I graduated with a bachelor's degree. That bachelor's degree studies had taken me more than four years to finish because I had to take more classes as a foreign language speaker. I felt tired, so I took a break for one year. After that year, in August 2019, I applied and registered to Northeastern Illinois University to pursue a master's degree program in the political science field. My gratitude to God, my family, and especially to my wife, Mimose O. Bacette, for supporting me and helping to graduate. I received my Master's Degree in Political Science, International Relations Sphere, at the age of fifty-five.

My gratitude also goes to Carmelitte Breton, who pushed me to return to school. She brought her support to me by assisting me with my basic needs. Her support was a source of encouragement to motivate me to go to work and go to school at the same time. From this moment, I want to let her know that her motivation and support made me achieve a higher level of education. While the same motivation also manifested to support her to achieve the unexpected position in her last professional job position.

The politologue Vilio Bacette encourages people of all ages to continue their education to change their life, because "knowledge is power," which is the key to success. Indeed, the grace of school politologue Vilio Bacette has the potential to think, share, teach, and bring his academic support to his community and the world.

Photos

Carmellitte B. Nestor, my mentor and supporter

Mimose Bacette, my wife, is on the right, and Nathalie Sylvestre, the stepmother of my younger son, Rodolf Jim Bacette, is in the middle on my graduation day.

This is my status with the International Organization for Migration.

This is my daughter and my last child, Farah Cathy Bacette. Farah helped with the technology I needed to do my presentation online. Thank you so much, Farah.

The politologue is thinking about the perspective of the United Nations to exterminate the world and especially black countries.

My graduation with a bachelor's degree in political science

Salutation and reception of the honorary diploma

Vilio Bacette and Mimose O. Bacette

Undergraduate Vilio Bacette

Vilio's graduation day

Vilio Bacette

Vilio Bacette

The observation of the United Nations during its evil agenda to destroy Haiti and strip it of its pride and dignity. The absence of representation of black countries as permanent members of the Security Council makes the UN an asymmetrical organization.

Graduate student Vilio Bacette

INTRODUCTION

Currently, the world suffers all sorts of pathogens and pandemic diseases, political crises, inflation, and economic depression that are linked to human and natural disasters. Those social calamities occurred due to the mismanagement of world affairs.

To prevent violations of human rights and secure security and peace, world leaders created the UN. The superpowers monitor the international organization's attempts to provide all countries and their citizens the same levels of dignity, integrity, and goods and service.

CHAPTER 1

∞

History of the First Haitian Immigrants to Chicago

Chicago was founded by Jean Baptiste Point-DuSable, a Haitian, and Chicago has the third-largest economy of all cities in the United States, but the presence of Haitians in the city has not made an influential impact on the city.

The first Haitian immigrants arrived in Chicago in 1960, during the totalitarian reign of the Duvalier regime. Duvalier employed terror to establish his dominance and government. The administration pushed the political elite out of the country, and Haitians of many other categories who opposed his totalitarian regime were exiled. Most immigrated to Africa, Canada, and other places in the US in addition to Chicago.

Haitians wanting to immigrate to Chicago required sponsors. Students were among the first to go to Chicago on scholarships provided by the regime. Other groups decided to stay in Haiti and work as secret agents, and others came to Chicago to work as domestic labor, factory workers, taxi drivers, hotel workers, and other positions of labor.

American Educational System

Most Haitians who were born in the US did not speak Creole as a second language. Haitian children who came to the US at a certain age were integrated into the existing educational system, which banned parents from speaking Creole at home because the schools taught English as a

1

second language. The schools wanted the children to practice English at home, and some families did not want their children to speak Creole for various reasons including their lack of education, their ignorance about the benefits of being bilingual, and cultural abandonment. The main reason some Haitian families abandoned their mother language was that they considered it inferior, which was wrong; no language is inferior to any other. But due to that, they preferred to speak English instead of Creole. Their lack of education deprived their children of becoming bilingual, a resource for members of ethnic groups.

Ignorance about Being Bilingual

Ignorance about bilingualism leads to a loss of cultural benefits. Individuals and ethnic groups that speak several languages have a greater capacity to progress economically. English, French, and Spanish add to a national language and expand a community's ability to communicate, and that increases excellent international relations between nations. Those who are bilingual find opportunities to use that ability for instance in translating one language to another.

Cultural Abandonment

Some cultural abandonment was due to the fact that many Haitian immigrants had been victims of a totalitarian regime. They decided to drop all their Haitian traditions and identification; the atrocities being committed in that country were very cruel. Lacking all respect for human rights, the regime brutally killed many people, including children.

The massacre of fourteen people in April 1963 tried to justify these brutal killings. One survivor of the Duvalier regime had a chance to leave the country with her son, and she took him with her to the airport to leave. At the airport, an agent of the regime put out his cigar in her son's face, and there was nothing she could do about it; she just cried and fled the country. That kind of behavior pushed many to abandon their country and all its traditions. They saw Haiti as a country of terror, and they wanted to forget everything about it including the language.

Evolution

Despite the challenges they faced, the first generation of Haitian immigrants to Chicago evolved and created a stable community of workers. With their wages and their new immigration status, they were able to sponsor their relatives in Haiti to come to Chicago. The second generation of immigrants enlarged the community and integrated into society.

Some of them made significant progress in the system and gained some access to intercede for Haiti and improve the allure of the community. But some Haitian scholars determined that the second generation ignored Haiti's calamity and were not a true Haitian community in Chicago. Most observers thought that it was normal to have a lack of structure in the Haitian community there.

The first generation was not intellectually or financially able to build a Haitian social structure in Chicago; they thought that Chicago was too far for other Haitians in the US to travel to. Another school of thought argued that it did not matter how many Haitians lived in the same community because it would expand. They thought it was important to create a cultural, ethnic base. It would accommodate a physical place to work together and to establish an institution as a legacy for all Haitian generations.

A Political Clash of Generations

The old arrival generation, which comprised Haitians who came in 1960, and the new arrival generation, whose members arrived in 1990, engaged in political controversy. The new generation accused the old arrivals of being generally idiotic, conservative, and corrupt. The discord occurred because the older generation had not built any infrastructure to help orient the new arrivals, and the two generations quarreled about that.

There were no social organizations such as schools or cultural and sports clubs that could welcome and assist the new arrivals. The older generation organized entertainment including some nightclub events. They invited musical groups from Haiti, New York, Canada, and other places to perform. These events consisted of Haiti's customs, and several bands played in different locations every weekend from Friday to Sunday. Fans supported their favorite bands and dances as people did in Haiti, but those kinds of cultural events almost disappeared.

Soccer is Haitians' favorite sport. Several professional soccer players resided in the community including Manes Cherestal (Ballon Manes) and Edner Sauveur (Malia). The young Haitian soccer players created teams to compete with each other.

But the Haitian community did not teach Haitian values to the new generation. The lack of schools pushed Haitian children to be monolingual while other ethnic groups had at least two languages. Therefore, Haitian children were less competitive. In addition, Haitian parents were prejudiced against their own language and abandoned it in favor of French and English, which deprived their children of the advantages of being bilingual and thus being more competitive.

The lack of social activities, which could have strengthened the Haitian community, disappointed those who knew how a community must be built. Nonetheless, there was no formal institution to develop a Haitian community in Chicago, and unfortunately, there are still no plans to do so.

The Failure

The integrative generation thus made a tremendous negative impact. It identified itself as American rather than Haitian. They did not construct any durable social structures such as organizations, foundations, centers, literary clubs, patriotic activities, or cooperative businesses.

What they tried to create was only temporary; it could not succeed because it was based on mediocracy, favoritism, and prejudice, which do not promote harmony in any community in terms of the creation of businesses and opportunities for socialization. Those negative behaviors generated intense quarrels and hindered the functioning of that entity. At the same time, the dissolution of the organization became automatic because education and training were neglected as practical tools to run an institution.

Education, Structure, and Methodology

Three elements were needed to prevent the dissolution of the Haitian community. First, education—the key to creating any organization. Education promotes the development of essential organizational elements such as ideology, objectives, and goals. Institutional doctrine can then direct whatever an organization promotes whether it is political, economic, or cultural in nature, and it keeps it in line with its objectives. The more knowledge one acquires, the easier one finds it to achieve success, create activities, change structures, and make improvements.

The Haitian community could have encouraged people to work together on specific societal projects. The leaders and the followers needed to form and inform each other on how to socialize, to work together, to be tolerant, and to be constantly on the same page so that they could achieve their goals. Equally important, the formation of the members needed to be the sine qua non.

Education includes taking appropriate courses, seminars, retreats, and general meetings with guest speakers who address crucial topics including prejudice, racism, and finances. Those kinds of activities democratize an organization's vital structure.

Structure

Second, there was no structure to create a Haitian community. The creation of an organization is a constitutive act; it requires a mission statement to declare its existence. It follows the organization's constitution and internal policies. It makes up an organization's skeleton or backbone. These policies establish the chain of execution, the organization's head and body members including the executive branch, committees, commissions, and a general assembly. The mission statement of the organization determines the creation of those entities. And the organization must have criteria for elections. It has to be defined and put in place so members can officially implement the organization's structure and goals.

Methodology

Methodology is a criterion that consists of an institution's plan of attack. It is constituted of the policies that help it realize short-, medium range-, and long-term projects. The method is a manner of approaching a proposal, an idea; it is an action plan. Developing a methodology requires the time, savoir-faire, and punctuality on the part of an organization's members.

Timing is a severe matter for Haitian organizers and participants, but Haitians are not likely to be on time. They can organize significant events such as meetings and festivities such as national holidays and impromptu events, and they show up and participate in those events, but they rarely arrive or leave on time, a constant dilemma for their compatriots. Not being on time for meetings or events generates laziness, discouragement, and dysfunction in an organization. That is behavior the Haitian people must correct in their social activities.

CHAPTER 2

∞

Unsuccessful Haitian Businesses

The Haitian community includes professionals in diverse fields who can improve its financial well-being, but the lack of organic structures such as a Haitian chamber of commerce that could support entrepreneurs intellectually and professionally harm its financial potential.

Haitian businesses face barriers. Haitian businesspeople are typically a marginalized group. According to some scholars, in terms of skin color, 97 percent of Haitians have black skin and 3 percent have lighter skin. Therefore, Haitian business owners face financial obstacles such as a lack of access to loans. The existence of a chamber of commerce could reduce some racial and economic barriers.

The mobility of cash in a community contributes to its financial growth; it allows owners of businesses to profit and then put that money into developing projects including parks and sports fields that children in the neighborhood can enjoy. Their money can also be used to buy school supplies for the children and provide scholarships to talented children. This will prompt members of the community to support such businesses rather than buy what they need elsewhere.

Unfortunately, Haitian businesses have faded out progressively. In 1994, there were two business transfers, two beauty salons, one restaurant, one Haitian band called Custom Band, and some fragmented radio stations and TV shows. Azaka Ajanakou is a famous television presenter who was awarded by Chicago with a personal day in the city for his efforts and contributions to the Haitian community.

It was a social catastrophe to have many churches in the tiny community. Most religious leaders were not qualified to be pastors, and some were simply self-proclaimed pastors who rose to the ranks of evangelists, predicators, deacons, and deputy pastors in tiny rooms they used as churches. Their mediocrity was the common denominator in the community. As a result, the community remains undeveloped without many economic resources. Nowadays, most of those activities have disappeared considerably.

CHAPTER 3

Haitian Competitiveness with Other Ethnic Communities

Haitian American Community Center

Lack of vision and selfishness allowed the closure of the center, which was a focal point for Haitians in Illinois.

Community centers can play important roles for Haitians in terms of promoting the language, the flag, monuments like the Citadelle, the seventh marvelous of the world, religion, dance, and food. A center is a diminutive nation-state that represents the nation abroad. The center is responsible for informing those who want to visit Haiti and sharing data about its history, customs, and current state in terms of the cataclysms that hit the country from time to time, for instance, earthquakes, hurricanes, explosions, and armed gangs created by the international community. Indeed, that center has the fundamental mission to represent the nation to the world. It is the home base of the Haitians who live in Illinois and especially Chicago.

The Haitian Center in Chicago

The center is now closed, which means that Haitians cannot receive any assistance from it. It is a horrible situation to face while the assistants are not available to help people defend or protect themselves. In the US, immigrants face many challenges including their immigration status,

9

family scandals, child molesters, and diverse social calamities that can occur to obligate the center to intervene as a moral and cultural entity. Most of the time, mature people and the US culture can countenance a criminal offense for killing, raping, stealing, and scandals involving minors. They can be indicted for that while that person is not involved in that scandal. Therefore, the center can intervene to reduce the cause and effect of that litigation.

Two significant problems victimize our compatriots—they do not speak English, and they cannot represent themselves. Notwithstanding, the existence of a structural center makes one feel that there is no ethnic group without a legal home base in a community center.

Haitian American Community Association (HACA)

The first generation of Haitians in Chicago created the HACA, the Haitian American Community Association. It seems that it had only short-term objectives and a limited mission to help people who faced language barriers. The center was closed several times after the founder's death, but others legally reinstated it. The center reactivated the refugees' arrival in 1992 from Guantanamo Bay, the US military base in Cuba. Unfortunately, the center is now closed due to the pandemic and other socioeconomic obstacles the community faces, and newcomers who could benefit from it are still arriving.

The center is a nonprofit with a 501(c)(3) status. That allows it to survive with the financial, human, and material resources it receives from individuals and city, state, and federal programs even though the center cannot get one of those programs to provide services to the community for some people and create jobs for others. The center lost that opportunity due to the lack of qualified staff.

The staff of the HACA is selected primarily by personal relationships, which means that some of the staff lack competence. The mediocracy of the staff decreases the dignity of the Haitian community while it increases its hypocrisy and shame. The community includes some high-level intellectuals, professionals, and elected officials, but they leave the center to be led by those without the academic knowledge to run an ethnic institution. The center's staff represents themselves as high-ranking intellectuals.

Some critics argue that it is a shame for the Haitian elite to live in a community without research, an academic formation, and a structural frame. The poorly educated staff who run the center has merit because it intends to do something while the eminent scholars do not channel their efforts toward developing a civilized and modernized center. They are more mediocre, repugnant, and ignorant than the people who want to conduct the center in their own way, which reduces the community's self-esteem.

The Dysfunctional Haitian Congress

The Haitian Congress to Fortify Haiti (HCFH) is another community organization that had the virtue of changing the allure of HACA and other Haitian religious, professional, and pressure groups in Chicago and other areas of the Midwest. That momentum dropped when the congress could not become an umbrella entity for other organizations. The goal of the HCFH is to create a mother organization that would coordinate Haitian activities in the regions and give support to Haitians and Haiti.

The HCFH was a new and powerful ideological organization in Illinois. It reunifies all Haitians regardless of their backgrounds or professional, academic, ideological, or political views. HCFH's idea was apparent in the mind of certain observers, partisans, and members, but it became opaque while the project had some financial support to launch. Gradually, to create the organization, community meetings were held so people could voice their concerns and expel externalities and reduce social obstacles.

That theme had been debated over and over before the creation of the organization. The primary concern was trust and respect because many people were victims of predators. The abuse of confidence was repetitive in the community. The strong tried to take advantage of the weak. That was why there was an untrusting attitude in the community. People who were victims of abuse of confidence and fraud were skeptical about the behavior of their compatriots who had engaged in fraudulent acts, and the issue was put on the table to discuss and resolve for reconciliation and to get back the trust of the Haitian community.

Haitians were so proud to have the organization that addressed social issues and built up their confidence. It was a victory for Joyce to develop an organization that would deal with social, economic, cultural, and political issues.

The Name of the Haitian Congress

The organization's name is a mistake because it cannot measure the efforts and sacrifices that gave credit to its name. It was a farce to give that name to a new organization. We Haitians do not consider ourselves a united people legally or democratically. The US Congress is a legislative branch of the US government; another entity that calls itself a congress has its ideology, strategy, and respect to move forward, and it is almost a state entity. Some concerned compatriots had some doubts about that name, but the majority voted in its favor. The catastrophe that happened to the congress is now nonexistent in terms of the umbrella.

The Status of the Haitian Congress

The chapter of the Haitian Congress created a gap among the board members. The chapter previewed eleven members who constituted the executive board and five members for the executive branch. The five members overrode the six members, which was in the majority. There was confusion between the executive branch and the rest of the members.

The confusion was that the executive branch took orders from the majority, which voted in favor of the resolution and authorized the executive branch to execute the order to whom it may concern. What if the president makes it done, the treasurer makes it done, and so on. The executive branch took the initiative without the majority's approval. That correlates with a massive gap in the organization that caused the failure of the Haitian Congress.

The Haitian Congress's nonprofit status allowed it to accept donations and gifts and hold fundraisers to finance itself and its projects.

Two sad events prompted the organization to solicit donations. The first was the earthquake that hit on January 12, 2010. It took the lives of 3,000 and injured 5,000 injured, and an unknown number of others just disappeared, so the exact number of victims is unknown. Property damage was extreme. The cataclysm was so egregious that people everywhere mobilized to support the Haitian victims. Compatriots sent goods and money to the congress to distribute to the victims. The amount of money is unknown, and the goods were not distributed equally. Some critics assumed that $100,000 was collected to assist the victims but that the congress's board members met to find a better way of spending the money to help the victims.

A proposition was made that the board could best support the victims by helping them relaunch their activities. Of the $100,000, $1,000 could go to each of the seventy primary victims who would be chosen by the congress, which would submit their names to Fond Coze. Cooperative financial organizations would monitor the fund, and the interest it earned would be distributed to the second wave of victims. That proposal had been denied. The congress missed a wonderful opportunity to impose its preponderance and establish its legacy in Haiti and among those in the diaspora. The loss of that momentum downgraded the effort and its dominance over believers, observers, and members of the congress. The donations dwindled, and people were skeptical about sending contributions to the congress because the critics argued that the methodology the congress used to spend the money was inaccurate.

A New Paradigm for Perfect Modernization

The congress has to change its model of operation and manner of spending so that it could create a new paradigm for the congress. Money has to be spent the way that donors desire it to be spent, and they have to be satisfied with the accounting. Confident organizers collect money and use it for purposes different from those they ask the donors to contribute to. That comportment hurts the feelings of the people financially. The outcome is that the organization has meager income to finance its budget. Therefore, the new paradigm became necessary for the organization to generate money to fuel its budget.

The new paradigm is to educate, form, disseminate, share information, and have experience in general management, development, and the monitoring of the funds. To manage a public or private entity, the leitmotiv is knowledge. The primary key is the formation of the members, the sanctuary for the elderly members, and ongoing formation for the leaders. That means that diverse spheres should relate to the nature of the organization including its social, professional, economic, cultural, and political aims. Knowledge and obeying all the rules can overcome mismanagement.

The congress must follow this new model that focuses on continuous formation and the dissemination of information.

Contributions of Certain Personalities

Some critics observed the massive contributions confident local Haitian leaders made to improve the effectiveness of the Haitian community. Numerous leaders sacrificed themselves to create different couloirs of concertation to find a formula to unite the several clans and lead them to construct a durable consensus to develop the community. A few of them are Politologue Vilio Bacette, Dr. Joel Augustin, Clement Papillon, Robert Pressoir, Martine Theodor, Anthony Vogel, Harry Fouche, Emile Andre, Ketlie Acacia, Henry Claude Gedeon, Dr. Jean Alexandre, Azaka Adjanakou, Patrick Augustin, Ancien Pierre Antoine Sylvestre, Edner Franck. Those people work into different spheres to corporately make dreams become a reality.

Vilio Bacette

Vilio Bacette had practical experience working in social organizations in Haiti; with that knowledge, he shared his experience with several groups that wanted to be involved in helping those in need.

He served the Haitian American Community Center as a board member and treasurer for six years, and he participated in the foundation of and served on the board of the Haitian Congress to Fortify Haiti. He has contributed to Haitian media including radio shows and television programs.

Dr. Joel Augustin

Dr. Joel Augustin is a physician educated in Haiti who came to the US and worked as a physician. He attended medical school during the Duvalier era. He opposed the Duvalier regime; he wanted the regime to act democratically.

Dr. Augustin is a proactive leader who wants to change the country and create a new life for all Haitians in terms of their political rights. He is involved in various civic movements to change Haitians' conditions and bring structural change to Haiti. Among other things, he inaugurated the Haitian Congress to Fortify Haiti and was an elected and effective secretary of the congress and later its president. Later, he created the Midwest organization, and now, he runs the unified fund of Haiti in the diaspora. Dr. Augustin enters a prominent political position that thinks for loot for a durable solution to the long-standing Haitian crisis.

Clement Papillon

Clement Papillon, who died a long time ago, was a pioneer in the Haitian community and the founder of the Haitian Center. He opened the center to assist Haitian immigrants become settled. Some contemporaries argue that Papillon was a handful to run the center financially. Unfortunately, one Papillon opened the Haitian Center and another Papillon closed it.

Critics accused Papillon and his staff of running the center with mediocrity and selfishness. The community did not support the center because of its policy imposed to conduct the identity communal. The dilemmas were unfair elections, unqualified officials, irregular services, and lack of programs.

Caisse Robert Pressoir

Caisse Robert Pressoir rescued the center's legal papers from 1990 when someone tried to put them in the trash because the center had a long-standing history of passivity and inactivity. Pressoir was the president of the center in 1994. He decided to reinstate the center so it could assist those in need. During his administration, a significant scandal occurred while he had his business in the same building as the center.

Henry Claude Gedeon, a member of the administration, was disciplined by Martine Theodore, the director of the center, who held up his check. People who witnessed his work for the community said that he was an incredible advocate for the Haitian community. Gedeon accused the staff that used the Social Security numbers of the refugees to collect from the agency in the name of certain refugees. That allegation generated a mass protest among the center clientele. The board members resigned, and the center ran under new staff members. Some other concerned people asked for a financial report that Robert and Martine refused to provide. The United Way canceled its contributions to the center because of its lack of transparency.

Martine Theodore

Martine Theodore was the director of the center who ran the center perfectly before the scandal. In that scandal, people revealed that the money of the center was misused under Martine's leadership. After the tragic drama, the center continued to exist miserably.

Anthony Volel

Anthony Vogel was a political activist in the Haitian community during the coup d'état against Jean Bertrand Aristide, a constitutionally and democratically elected president in a credible and honest Haitian election. Volel commentated the news on a Haitian radio program, Radio Soleil, hosted by Robert Pressoir and Martine Theodore to inform the Haitian community. Later on, Volel became the treasurer of the Haitian Center. After a severe quarrel in the center, Volel resigned and opened his own center, which faced some difficulties and closed.

Harry Fouche

Harry Fouche is a political leader who was discovered during the plot against President Jean Bertrand Aristide in September 1991. He engaged in mass protests to ask for the reinstatement of democratic order in Haiti. The mass protests included marches, sit-ins, radio shows, and meetings to mobilize Haitians to return to a democratic form of government.

Fouche, an economist, gave a series of radio interviews over Voice of America to maintain the mobilization for the return of democracy. At the same time, the military putschists intensified the massacres, and the protest movements weakened. Voice of America announced a march in Washington organized by Chicago supporters led by Fouche that fueled the campaign that energized the militants in Haiti.

Fouche became general council in New York after President Aristide returned to power for a second term. He worked with the Haitian community and other minority groups that had issues identical with the Haitians' issues. His contributions to the Haitian community have improved its situation tremendously.

Emile Andre

Activist Emile Andre worked closely with Fouche to conscientize people about the crimes in Haiti, and he took a stand against torture, physical abuse, rape, imprisonment, and killings. Those acts constituted crimes against humanity that the Hague Treaty had prohibited. Those civic movements reduced the military atrocities and the evil attempts of the UN to expel the Haitian society, a black nation.

Andre hosted a radio show at Loyola University's radio station called Radio L'Union every Saturday from 4:00 to 6:00 p.m. with co-hosts. Andre was the vice-consul at the Haitian consulate in Chicago. His contributions to the Haitian community were greatly appreciated.

Keltie Acacia

Keltie Acacia is a professional woman who worked in the social science field for human resources in Illinois. She dedicated herself to helping others and particularly Haitians. She was the vice-chair of the Haitian Community Center Association, and she was involved in different social aspects and circumstances including public aid in the form of food stamps, Medicaid, housing, and court translations. She organized social and health events at the center with her team for disease treatment and prevention. She continues to contribute to the community; she became a member of the Haitian Congress. The Haitian community expressed its gratitude for her contributions to it.

Lynn Toussaint

Lynn Toussaint, a lawyer, worked for the Cook County public defender's office. She was chair of the Haitian Community Center assisted by Keltie Acacia. She presided over the Haitian Congress and ran it for several terms. Lynn continues to advocate for the community. She was elected as trustee on the board of Oakton Community College, and she served several ethnic groups there for six years.

Confidence in Toussaint regressed when she gave her consent to the State Department to keep Jovenel Moise in power to organize a referendum and elections to change the Haitian Constitution. Some observers viewed that as an act of treason. Consequently, she ignored Haitian history and the asymmetric relationship with Haiti; it is the act of a traitor.

Henry Claude Gedeon

Henry Claude Gedeon was involved in public relations for the Haitian American Center Association (HACA). He served as a translator in court for Haitians, and he was responsible for picking up food and distributing it to people. His social services were helpful to the Haitian community.

Dr. Jean Alexandre

Jean Alexandre is a former Haitian ambassador to the UN and UNESCO. His contribution to the Haitian community is not public but is valid. Dr. Alexandre is a tacit political activist; he looks for immense socioeconomic change in Haiti.

Azaka Adjanakou

Azaka Adjanakou is a native Haitian born in Jeremie in the Grand-Anse Department. He changed his name to Azaka Adjanakou based on his cultural ideology. Azaka is known nationally as a TV show producer for CAN TV, a public TV station. His segment is called Unity, and diversity is life. He took charge of a group of refugees who arrived in Chicago to orient them and help them integrate into American society. Azaka helped out in various school, hospital, housing, and advisory cases.

Patrick Augustin

Patrick Augustin is a social worker in charge of the Haitian refugee in the Uptown Church office. Among his tasks, he was responsible for finding jobs for newcomers. Augustin developed a great relationship with the refugees and oriented them in a good direction. He merits the gratitude of the Haitian community.

Pierre Antoine Sylvestre

Pierre Antoine Sylvestre is the first elder in the Seventh Day Adventist Church in Evanston. He is active at the Haitian Center, and he hosted an evangelical radio show. Pierre Antoine Sylvestre, Jean Accel Ternier, Danielle Souffrant, Eugenie Franck, Natalie Sylvestre, Guerda Laguerre, and others belonged to the Seventh Day Adventist Church, and they all have assisted Haitians. Without such good Samaritans, the Haitian community would lack many social services. Their assistance was welcomed and recognized by the Haitian community.

Jean-Vil Joseph

Jean-Vil Joseph, an exceptional radio animator in Haitian entertainment, started in the 2000s. The Haitian community is involved in the media in the same era with specific radio and television segments. Most shows are played on public stations such as Evanston TV and CAN TV in Chicago. WONX broadcast most of the segments. Later on, the radio changed ownership and stopped broadcasting Haitian shows, so Joseph decided to create a Haitian internet radio station, Radio La Différence, a well-equipped online radio station. However, with only one host and limited finances, the radio station has suffered.

Garry Gaspard

Gary Gaspared initiated the diffusion of Haitian music on the air. The intensification of radio programs occurred in 1990 after the overthrow of President Aristide. The Haitian people, especially the partisans of Lavalas, Aristide's party, mobilized a return to democracy. Therefore, more people were involved in the radio diffusion and created various programs such as the news from Haiti.

Edner Franck

Edner Franck worked in the sports domain and contributed enormously to the Haitian community. He created a soccer team in Chicago that played in Haiti; his players are considered ambassadors because they represent the country via soccer, Haiti's national sport. He channeled many youth into soccer.

Amplias Gabeau

Pastor Amplias Gabeau was one of several evangelical leaders in the Haitian community who exerted great effort to serve Haitian immigrants. He utilized his church to welcome those who had difficulty finding places to live and establishing themselves in the country. He is an excellent example of a true leader. Some of those compatriots acknowledged the humanitarian contribution that Pastor Gabeau brought to them. The Haitian community greatly appreciates his contributions to the Haitian community in Chicago.

Fenix Etienne

Fenix Etienne, Duclos Etienne and family, Roosevelt Saint-Vil, Boursiquot Mercius, and many others contributed to the Haitian community. Fenix Etienne teaches sociology and is a public service leader who helps social organization leaders lead and achieve their goals and provide the members with the formation and information they need to succeed. Etienne came from the OIM organization in Chicago in 1994. He helped create a nonprofit organization and participated in some radio and television programs to change the social and cultural paradigm of Haitians in Chicago.

CHAPTER 4

Perspective of Politologue Vilio Bacette

Loss of Haiti

Toussaint Louverture, an experienced army general, was the precursor of Haiti's independence. He served in the French, Spanish, and British armies, and he returned to the French army as its general in chief. He also became governor of the French territory. In the end, Louverture was arrested by the French authorities and sent to France to die.

Haiti, the first independent black nation, has a remarkable military history in its battles against French attempts to establish its hegemony over the country. Haiti withstood many attempts to exterminate it as a country. Many Haitian patriots made great sacrifices to free the nation, whose independence was declared on January 1, 1804.

According to some historians, independence had not been planned; it was a revolt that involved two different but simultaneous actions. Historian Rene Julien explained that the Haitian army officers who served the French army in the colony were to be replaced by French officers who came from France to take command; the plan was to arrest the Haitian officers and send them to other regions in the Caribbean.

Dessalines, a Haitian officer, heard of this and reported the matter to Alexandre Petition, a French army officer, but Petition was one French officer who was to be arrested. The conversation had a significant impact on Haitian officers, who unified to fight that decision and prevent themselves from getting arrested and humiliated as had happened to Toussaint Louverture.

The concerned officers mobilized their troops and started a long battle with France that took place throughout Haiti and ended in a Haitian victory at a battle in Vertiere on November 18, 1804. After that, a protocol agreement was signed by the Haitian military and the French authorities. After the French left the country, there were no colonial authorities there. The Haitian authorities established the island of Hispaniola as the first black independent country in the world.

Haiti had a significant number of enemies; it was not welcome in the concert of nations. Instead of being honored by other countries, it was considered still a country of slaves. The principal enemies of Haiti are occidental countries, and the primary enemy is the US, which is hegemonic.

Haiti lost much of its natural resources to countries that called themselves friends of Haiti, which was a lie. Certain countries grabbed Haiti's mineral resources by force without any official agreements. Their actions destroyed Haiti's socioeconomic and agricultural landscape.

The US invaded Haiti in 1915 and occupied it against the will of the Haitians. There was no evidence of any violence, war, or genocide in Haiti that encouraged a form of R2P intervention at that period. The invasion by the US was meant to seize Haiti's financial assets valued at $1 million in spite of that being contrary to international treaties.

The agricultural industry was devastated, and the country's religions and customs were altered. During the invasion, mediocre territory management left a hole in the second occupation in 1945 with the same scenario. Those occupations purposed were the reestablishment of slavery.

The historians related that during those two horrible periods, there were many assassinations and attempts at genocide; people were massacred based on their skin color and economic status; many lost their possessions without compensation. Many observers cried out against such crimes and violations of international treaties perpetrated by a hegemonic state that was obligated to protect small, poor states. Many Haitians were imprisoned, murdered, or exiled, which resulted in a great reduction of the number of professionals and intellectuals who could have improved the country's status. This all happened because Haiti was too close to the United States.

Restore Haiti

Restoring Haiti will not be simple, but it could occur if Haitians created a consensus and a social contract for at least fifty years to change the political paradigm. That new paradigm must consist of the church closing, redefining the Vienna Treaty, repatriating state services, reestablishing state stores, and stopping corruption and stealing. The state's resources have to be distributed legally and equally to the nationals so that their fundamental needs are met.

Religions

Islam

Churches are remarkable organs that can publicize the ideology of a system, which could be a mafia group or a sociopolitical regime. Those systems utilize churches to mobilize people by brainwashing them into submitting to any policy and action. Evidently, the terrorist group ideology is based on Islam; they commit their acts that resulted in repatriating the lands that pertained to Allah. The leading technique that militant terrorist groups use is violence and killing in God's name. Nonetheless, after cruel massacres, the militants go to church to pray and return to the street to continue their deceit. What kind of God takes pleasure in the shedding of innocent blood?

Muslims are willing to become martyrs to serve Allah. They think that they will go to heaven even after committing criminal acts, that God will give them seventy-two women there, and that they can choose family members to live with them. To be cited,

Christianity

Similar to that, the imperialist system uses Christianity to exploit people. All religions have doctrines and methods of assembly in churches. The church's leadership includes pastors, committees, deacons, preachers, and congregations. That structure has an allure of integrity, truth, and perfection. The system upholds the Bible as its foundational document. The objective is to make people believe in its superfluous fiction including Jesus Christ. The Bible is a spiritual constitution for Christians.

Nowadays, there are sixty-six books in the Bible, but at the beginning, there were four—Luke, Mark, John, and Matthew as adopted by Constantine in 325 at the Laodicean council that established religious rules because there were too many of them and were unorganized. Research demonstrates that several books including Judas, Pierre, Thomas, and Marie Madeleine Evangile were not included in the Bible for political reasons.

The goal of Muslims and Christians is to gain eternal life in heaven after they die. The cult of Islam focuses on the prophet Muhammad. Both religions developed in the Middle East. Christians believe that after they ascend to heaven, they will have a pleasurable time meeting Jesus Christ and worshipping God without distractions. Families and sex will play no roles in heaven. The voice is the only channel of identification because salvation is personal. Christianity does not encourage Christians to focus on their lives on earth and to earn money but on their eternal reward in heaven. The Bible is meant to wash people's brains to the detriment of others. That is imperialism.

The imperialist system is a horrible system for developing countries. The system divides the world economy into two financial entities—the global north and the global south. The global north countries consist of rich countries while the global south encompasses emerging countries. The global north countries have accumulated three-quarters of the planet's resources and exclude the majority of marginalized people from them. That selfish behavior causes many to live in profound poverty, starvation, and disease.

Poverty

The global north countries are invulnerable to pandemics while the global south countries suffer from viruses with multiple hosts to reproduce with unexpected rapidity due to insufficient food, polluted water, lack of health care, low incomes, poor housing, and degraded environments. Those facts are human vulnerabilities that make them hosts for many viruses. The rich countries have to let underdeveloped countries overcome those socioeconomic issues, diminish poverty, and stop the next generation of world pandemic threats.

Starvation

The lack of food can cause brain damage affecting organisms and cause systemic organ dysfunction. As a result, the immune system is attacked and develops several diseases. Former US president Bill Clinton promoted the exportation of Haitian rice to the US, which caused famine in Haiti. That act constituted a severe violation of human rights. Consequently, the economy of the planters disappeared, which pushed them into poverty. At this moment, the Food and Agriculture Organization (FAO) of the UN announced that 4.5 million Haitians could die of starvation.

Disease

More pandemics can occur due to the disparity in the socioeconomic situations between global north and global south countries. Third World countries, the so-called emerging countries, are victims of the imperial system by which the rich becoming richer and the poor becoming poorer. Rich countries manipulate the earth's resources for their benefit, but they construct socioeconomic issues to keep multiethnic groups of color and global south people in deep poverty, which causes people to lead unhygienic lives that can make them vulnerable to viruses and bacteria that can become worldwide threats.

There is some systematic confusion. The global north countries harmed the world in several ways that cruelly affected the poor in emerging countries. In contrast, they recognized and promoted Christianity against abuse, exploitation, and hatred and preached values such as the sharing goods, the protection of life, and the supporting of each other.

Individualism

The philosophy of Christianity is to divide people by preaching individuality, not communism. For instance, salvation is a personal matter. That regional paradigm is a constructed mindset that establishes individualism. To construct a real economy that is economically successful, entrepreneurs need financial assistance from their families or banks. Christianity teaches personal life, personal interest, not the collective interest, to help each other succeed financially. Even the family is divided. The family cannot go to heaven together. At the same time, Christianity teaches that the family is the foundation of society. The Bible says that a man has to leave his mother and father to live with his wife and create a family. However, only those who follow God's will will be saved and go to heaven. Otherwise, all family members must perish. It is a paradox to be in a family on earth but be single in heaven.

National Institutions

The three branches of the state must be balanced and symmetrically collaborated but must have complete independence from each other in the same way that Montesquieu related in the spirit of the law. This independence and interdependence has to exist to make the state accountable to its citizens and not subject them to a reign of partiality, corruption, and nepotism.

The Ministry of Culture must review, regulate, and eliminate religions in the country because they constitute a source of discord, hatred, prejudice, and discrimination. Churches must close for a structural review and recertification. That recertification consists of evaluating the mental capacity of the spiritual leaders, the ideology of the religion, and their relation to Haitian mythology, traditions, customs, and its constitution.

Hegemonic states use religion to brainwash believers into submitting to extreme poverty by giving them false hopes and untruth. That Evangile sits on the three angels' message that the church leaders called it, which is based on Jesus Christ's creation. The phenomenon of creation is a spiritual construct for a mission statement to force people to practice resilience and wait for the spectacular return of Jesus Christ. Those who have faith in that statement believe that Jesus Christ will deliver them from their socioeconomic dilemma that religion and spiritual leaders impose on them. Therefore, leaders institute ignorance, corruption, exploitation, and lies to maintain the believers' conditions of poverty. Churches divide the nation, reduce state performance, bring acculturation, and own the most agricultural lands. Religion has to be recertified and preach patriotism, unity, and love here on earth instead of a promise of heaven.

CHAPTER 5

The Creation and Failure of the United Nations

Creation of the UN

The United Nations was created on October 24, 1945, to promote global peace and security. The UN was dominated by the five permanent (P5) members of the Security Council, that maintained veto rights over the UN. The P5 dominated and violated UN policy and treaties that were signed and ratified by 189 other members. The P5 is free to create panic in the world with or without the approval of the UN, and that could lead to a third world war. For instance, the conflict between Russia and Ukraine is evidence of the laissez-faire attitude of the UN that spoils the US. Sadly, it is nonsense that the US attacked Iraq unfairly. Asymmetrically, the Russian attack on Ukraine is the other side of the coin that indicts the UN for its passivity.

The UN and NATO

Paradoxically, it is an ideological controversy. As an influential member of the P5 and the creator of the UN, the US caused confusion when it created NATO. The UN promotes peace and security in the world while NATO was founded by the US and Canada to wage war against the Soviet Union. With the creation of NATO, did the US and Canada revoke the UN?

CHAPTER 6

∞

Meisler's Exploration of the United Nations

We will explore Meisler's book, which focuses on the UN, a remarkable international institution that plays a significant role in protecting humanity in many ways. The book gives a general overview of the secretaries-general of the UN and of several agencies and its peacekeeping and peacemaking missions, resolutions, and treaties.

The UN was founded on October 24, 1945. The US, France, the UK, Russia, China, and other countries decided to create an international entity stronger than the League of Nations. That entity had a mission statement to promote peace and security. Meisler wrote,

> The Americans proposed that five permanent members with a veto and a few other rotating delegates make up a security council with authority to maintain international peace and security. Unlike the League of Nations, which had the power only to impose sanctions by unanimous vote, this Security Council could use "any means necessary." (28)

Creation of the United Nations

The UN struggled to develop a mission statement; a compromise had to be reached by all parties to create constitutive documents for the UN. Nonetheless, some discordant notes entered the symphony, which created disputes among the delegates. Meisler wrote,

The United Nations was forged in a pair of extraordinary conferences—at Dumbarton Oaks from late August to early October 1944 and at San Francisco from late April to late June 1945. The Dumbarton Oaks conference was limited in numbers but not power. Only Britain, Russia, the United States, and China took part. (16)

The crucial issue of the Dumbarton Conference was to determine the power of the powerful states including their veto power over UN decisions. Meisler wrote,

> But the real issue of the San Francisco conference was the same that plagued Dumbarton Oaks—the veto of the Big Five. Although the Soviet Union had agreed to the American formula at Yalta, Molotov now insisted that the formula meant that any of the Big Five could veto even the discussion of a dispute: a public debate over a dispute was too significant to be regarded as a procedural matter not subject to veto. (30)

After a critical discussion over the veto rights, five powerful countries agreed and gave birth to the UN.

> The United States served as the repository for the formal instruments of ratification. The first country to officially deposit the formal documents with the United States was the United States itself on August 8. Charter would "come into force," according to Article 110 when all of the Big Five and a majority of the rest deposited their ratifications. That happened on October 24, 1945, when the Soviet Union, Ukraine, White Russia, and Poland (finally admitted to the UN) handed their ratifications to the United States at the same time. James F. Byrnes, the new secretary of state, certified that all the requirements of Article 110 had been satisfied. "The United Nations Charter is now a part of the law of nations," he said.

October 24 would be celebrated each year as the UN's birthday. (33)

UN after Creation (Chapter 2 of Meisler's Book)

Trygve Lie was the first official secretary-general of the UN. A lot of debate, compromise, negotiation, and consensus took place before the General Assembly voted for a secretary-general of the UN. Most of the disputes were between the permanent members because each wanted control over the secretary-general to impose their plans and ideas and exercise their power. Meisler wrote,

> On January 29, 1946, the eleven-member Security Council, meeting in London, unanimously selected Trygve Lie, the forty-nine-year-old foreign minister of Norway, as the first secretary-general of the United Nations, a choice swiftly ratified by the General Assembly. (34)

There was some sentiment in the General Assembly to locate the UN permanently in Philadelphia or San Francisco. President Truman offered the use of the old Spanish fortress known as the Presidio in San Francisco without cost. Nevertheless, the Russians and British rejected San Francisco as too far from Europe. Trygve Lie favored New York and appealed to Mayor William O'Dwyer and Robert Moses, New York's urban planner and overseer of construction, to come up with an offer. Moses suggested the Turtle Bay area, six blocks of slaughterhouses and slums alongside the East River in central Manhattan. The cost was too high for the UN, but Moses began soliciting donations. On December 11, 1946, UN Ambassador Warren Austin, the former senator from Vermont who succeeded Stettinius, informed the UN that John D. Rockefeller Jr. had offered it $8.5 million to buy the Turtle Bay slum area. The General Assembly accepted the offer by a vote of forty-six to seven. The UN complex, including the thirty-nine-story Secretariat Building, the General Assembly Hall, and the Conference Building for the Security Council on eighteen acres of land, were designed mainly by Wallace K. Harrison, the architect for Rockefeller Center. With the work completed in less than six years, the UN settled into its own complex in 1952.

Ralph Bunche (Chapter 3)

US ambassador to the UN Ralph Bunche was never promoted to the position of secretary-general of the organization because he was a black man, but he made great contributions to it.

The principal told Nana that her grandson was such a good student that the teachers and staff had never thought of him as a Negro. "You are wrong to say that," replied Nana angrily. "It is an insult to Ralph, to me, to his parents and his whole race. Why haven't you thought of him as a Negro? He is a Negro, and he is proud of it. So am I." (48)

Bunche contributed to the UN, which led Israel to victory and independence; he was considered an Israel infant. Bunche was recognized as an international hero.

The Israelis also remembered that neither the UN nor any of its members had sent troops to defend the new state of Israel when it was invaded by the Arabs in 1948. In fact, in the view of the Israelis, the UN did not even try to stop the fighting until it was clear the Israelis would win. Yet Israel could not ignore the UN. The Arab-Israeli conflict would monopolize the attention of the young United Nations, only three years older than Israel itself, many times in its history, and Israel often had to bend to its will. Ralph Bunche returned to New

York, an international hero. Newspapers throughout the world credited him with bringing peace to the Middle East. (65)

Korean War (Chapter 4)

The Korean War was the first dilemma for Lie as secretary-general of the UN in 1950.

> Secretary-General Trygve Lie heard the phone ring around midnight Saturday, June 24, 1950. A radio newscast a few minutes earlier had reported skirmishing along the border separating North and South Korea, but the report had been too vague to fret over. The late-night caller was John Hickerson, assistant secretary of state for UN affairs, and he had more solid, more depressing news. He informed Lie that North Korean troops had invaded South Korea. "My God, Jack," said Lie, "that's the war against the United Nations." "Trygve, you're telling me," Hickerson replied. (66)

Lie did the best he could to resolve the Korean War. As a result, he got a resolution from the Security Council to condemn North Korea.

> The American resolution was adopted just before 6 p.m. by a vote of nine to nothing, with the Soviet Union absent and Yugoslavia abstaining. The resolution branded North Korea as guilty of a breach of peace, demanded an "immediate cessation of hostilities," ordered North Korea to withdraw its forces north of the thirty-eighth parallel, called on all members to help the UN carry out the resolution, and asked everyone to refrain from assisting the North Korean government. By that time, however, North Korea, claiming it had been invaded by Syngman Rhee's forces, had declared war on South Korea. (70)

Unfortunately, the Korean War ended with many casualties, injuries, and deaths.

> The casualties of the war were heavy, almost half coming after negotiations began after both sides had accepted that neither could win, that the war would end with two Koreas. The South Koreans had 415,000 soldiers killed and 429,000 wounded. The Americans recorded 33,629 dead and 105,785 wounded. British Foreign Secretary Anthony Eden, noting the heavy loss of American life, wrote later, "No just man will question the spirit of that sacrifice which bore no selfish taint." The British Commonwealth had 1,263 killed and 4,817 wounded. The rest of the UN forces suffered 1,800 deaths and 8,000 wounded. It has been estimated that between 500,000 and 1.5 million Chinese and North Koreans died in the fighting.

Being the secretary-general of the UN had its benefits but also some drawbacks, and the pressure took a big toll on Lie.

> On November 10, 1953, Lie shocked his chief aides with advance word of the news and then announced to the General Assembly that he was resigning as secretary-general and would remain in office only until the Security Council selected a successor. (83)

Dag Hammarskjöld (Chapter 5)

Dag **Hammarskjöld,** the new UN secretary-general, had to deal with a severe crisis between the US and China, both of which had veto powers in the UN, and Hammarskjöld had to find a compromise.

> On November 23, 1954, Peking Radio announced that a military court had convicted eleven US Air Force crewmen and two American civilians of espionage and sentenced them to prison terms ranging from four

years to live. The air force crew had been shot down in their B-29 bomber and the two civilians, presumably CIA agents, in their C-47 transport while flying over Manchuria during the Korean War. The CIA operatives were evidently attempting to drop Chinese Nationalist agents into Communist China, but the air force plane was on a routine mission spreading leaflets. The US government denied all the espionage charges, and the Chinese audacity infuriated the American public and politicians attempting to drop Chinese Nationalist agents into Communist China, but the air force plane was on a routine mission spreading leaflets. The US government denied all the espionage charges, and the Chinese audacity infuriated the American public and politicians. (94)

Hammarskjöld's efforts in handling the China crisis were successful.

In his memoirs, Eisenhower neglected to even mention Hammarskjöld in the chapter about the crisis with China over the offshore islands. Perhaps the Americans were right. But, for UN diplomats and officials, the dramatic trip to Peking and the release of the airmen had tested the mettle of Hammarskjöld and their own respect and admiration for him, and they now felt very good about their secretary-general. (101)

Suez Canal (Chapter 6)

The Israeli invasion and seizure of the Suez Canal, Egypt's property, created political tension between Israel and Egypt that the UN had to resolve.

At this instant, they are taking charge of the canal, the Egyptian canal, not the foreign canal—that canal that is on Egyptian territory, that crosses Egyptian territory,

that is a part of Egypt, and that is now the Property of
Egypt. (108)

In addition to that, the Security Council sometimes imposed its
will on the UN.

The Security Council suddenly sensed the depth of the
perfidy of the British and French. Israeli troops had
stormed across the Sinai Peninsula the day before to
join their paratroopers dropping near Suez while other
Israeli troops headed northward toward Ismailia on
the Suez Canal and southward toward the outpost of
Sharm el-Sheikh that blocked Israeli shipping through
the Gulf of Aqaba. (102)

Hammarskjöld's Suez Canal solution was a significant contribution
to the status of the UN.

The Settlement of the Suez crisis was one of the most
spectacular single achievements of the UN during its
history. In this crisis, unlike the Korean and Persian
Gulf Wars, the UN did not serve as a mere cloak for
American action. Moral condemnation by the United
Nations proved a powerful force. (120)

The Battles of Katanga and the Crash of Hammarskjöld (Chapter 7)

The African continent grappled with many issues including slavery, war,
rape, torture, and genocide due to the occupation of certain conquering
countries. Congo (now Zaire) was occupied by Belgium.

In July 1960, the United Nations dispatched the first
contingents of its Blue Helmets to the former Belgian
Congo [now Zaire] to restore law and order out of
bloody chaos and replace the Belgian troops who no
longer had any rightful place in an independent black
country. The UN had not mounted such a large and

audacious military force before. At Suez, the troops were performing what would become known as classic peacekeeping tasks—the impartial patrolling of cease-fire lines between belligerents who were content, for the time being, to avoid conflict. The Blue Helmets in Suez fired their arms only to protect themselves. The Congo operation would take the UN onto more dangerous ground. The Congolese people fight for their independence from Belgium because Belgium exploits Congo's natural resources, and mistreats the human resources, such as killings, embodied, and lack of knowledge.

Few colonies came to independence as unprepared as the Congo on June 30, 1960. Belgian colonialism had been harsh and exploitative. Out of a population of fourteen million, there were only seventeen black university graduates, not one a doctor, a lawyer, or an engineer. The hundred thousand Belgian settlers and bureaucrats ran the commerce and administration and expected to keep on doing so for years after independence. Unlike the British or the French, the Belgians provided no period of self-rule to prepare their colony for independence. (123)

Prime Minister Patrice Lumumba was a brave nationalist leader who wanted to change Congo when the country got its independence from Belgium and to repatriate the natural resources of the country from Belgium. The prime minister was arrested and assassinated, and later on, his wife was arrested and humiliated in the street.

The continent had many conflicts that contributed to making Africa unstable economically and politically; maybe that was the reason some scholars think that Hammarskjöld had failed.

The main casualty of the Congo was a grievous loss. Dag Hammarskjöld was awarded the Nobel peace prize for 1961 shortly after his death. For years, diplomats would insist that they were looking for another Dag Hammarskjöld whenever they scoured the lists of candidates for secretary-general. But, despite this insistence, they always seemed to choose someone who they were sure would give them far less trouble. (139)

Cuban Missile Crisis: The UN as Theater (Chapter 8)

The famous Bay of Pigs crisis created severe diplomatic tension and threatened to become an international war. The two superpowers confronted each other over the Bay of Pigs crisis, which was land the US leased from Cuba. When Cuba did not want to renew the lease, the US threatened to attack Cuba, and Cuba replied to the threat.

The CIA trained and equipped Cuban exiles at a camp in Guatemala and then led them in an amphibious landing on April 16 at the Bay of Pigs. The CIA painted Cuban air force markings on US B-26 bombers flown over Cuba by exile pilots from a field in Nicaragua to mask American involvement. These pilots, following a CIA cover story, were officially described as defectors from the Cuban air force turning on Castro. On April 15, when raids on Cuban airfields took place, one plane flew directly from Nicaragua to Florida to provide the cover story; a second, damaged over Cuba, flew to Florida as well because the pilot could not make it all the way back to Nicaragua. (145)

The US threatened to use nuclear weapons against the Soviet Union, but the two superpowers found a peaceful solution without the UN.

The most terrifying confrontation of the Cold War was settled by the two protagonists themselves. President Kennedy chose to deal with the crisis by threatening Khrushchev directly and threatening him with a nuclear war that the UN would have been powerless to prevent. (156)

U Thant and the Quest for Peace in Vietnam (Chapter 9)

Secretary-General U Thant, who followed Hammarskjöld, was elected to a five-year term. He failed to resolve the Nigerian war; according to him, it was an intranational war. Furthermore, he failed to end the Six Day War.

Despite the mounting deaths, he refused to intervene in the Nigerian civil war because it was an internal matter. And some analysts believe that the Six-Day War could have been averted if he had managed to hold the UN soldiers in place in the Sinai in the face of Nasser's demand that they go. (163)

The Vietnam War was very costly for the US in terms of material and human resources.

For almost twenty years, American governments preached that this was another Korea; if South Vietnam fell, the rest of Southeast Asia would fall to Communism like collapsing dominoes. President Kennedy committed almost 20,000 advisors and troops to the battle, and President Johnson escalated the number of troops until more than 550,000 Americans battled the Vietcong. By the time the war ended in 1975 with the defeat of the Americans and then the South Vietnamese, almost 60,000 Americans had died in Vietnam. Vietnamese casualties, of course, were far greater. (163)

The Six-Day War (Chapter 10)

U Thant pulled peacekeepers out of the Middle East whose purpose was to keep the Israelis and Egypt in check.

That leaves the place to Israel to take advantage of Egypt. Within two days of the Fawzi demand, Secretary-General U Thant shocked many world leaders by announcing the complete withdrawal of the emergency force (the first UN peacekeeping troops ever deployed). The decision was widely condemned at the time. With their buffer gone, nerves exacerbated, and rhetoric ever more fiery, the Israelis and the Arabs marched inexorably into another conflagration. Within three weeks, the Six-Day War erupted, ending in an astoundingly swift and overwhelming Israeli triumph—a victory, however, that turned bitter and onerous in the next quarter of a century and compounded the instability of the Mideast. (174)

The Arab-Israeli conflict would no longer occupy the UN as obsessively as it once did. The UN played a role during the 1973 Yom Kippur War when Egypt and Syria almost defeated Israel in a surprise attack. (186)

Kurt Waldheim: The Big Lie (Chapter 11)

Kurt Waldheim, a former Austrian army officer, was the next secretary-general.

In December 1971, when Kurt Waldheim of Austria was elected as the fourth secretary-general of the United Nations, his main rival was Max Jakobson of Finland, the first choice of the United States. But the Soviet Union had vetoed Jakobson, spreading the word it had done so because he was Jewish and thus unacceptable to the Arab world. In those days, it was known that Waldheim, like many other Austrians, had served as an officer in the German army during World War II. (188)

In the end, it came out that Waldheim had had connections to the Nazis.

Moynihan's wit would have metamorphosed into a fury if he had known the whole story. Waldheim had hidden most of it. He had joined two Nazi organizations during his youth. As a second lieutenant in World War II, he had been assigned to a German army unit in the Balkans that had rounded up thousands of Jews in Greece for deportation to Auschwitz and had killed thousands of innocent villagers in Greece and Yugoslavia as reprisals for attacks by the "Partisans," as Resistance fighters were known during the occupation. The commander, General Alexander Löhr, also an Austrian, had been executed as a war criminal after the war. The Yugoslav government had accused Waldheim as well of war crimes. The official document of the United Nations War Crimes Commission, charging Waldheim with "murder" and "putting hostages to death," was still in the rarely consulted archives of the UN. (189)

Zionism Is Racism (Chapter 12)

Women's rights remain controversial in spite of the many contributions women make to humanity. Some scholars say that women most of the time do better at their jobs than men do.

Zionism was a conference on women's equal rights organized by the UN, which had significant opposition among antifeminists.

Feminists had worked hard to persuade the UN to convene a women's conference and felt frustrated and angry over the prospect of its shriveling beneath a furious conflict that had nothing to do with women's issues. (206)

It follows that women's equal rights were granted after a long period.

It took sixteen years before the General Assembly would revoke the resolution branding Zionism a form of racism and racial discrimination. (221)

UNESCO: Defenses of Peace in the Minds of Men (Chapter 13)

UNESCO is a UN agency that promotes educational, scientific, and cultural organizations. As well, UNESCO manages the world's patrimony, the world's heritage.

> MacLeish, a former assistant secretary of state who had crafted the wonderful preamble to the U.N. Charter in San Francisco a few months earlier, wrote the opening lines of the UNESCO constitution as well: "Since wars begin in the minds of men; it is in the minds of men that the defenses of peace must be constructed." (222)

The US decided to leave UNESCO because it wanted the current secretary-general, M' Bow, to get a third term. But the different parties reached a consensus, and the US decided to return and applaud the job of UNESCO.

> UNESCO had become so marginal an agency for Americans that the significance of M'Bow's defeat and Mayor's election was little noted at the time. It was the strongest sign that the Cold War was coming to an end at the United Nations and that the Security Council could now start acting in a way that the founders of the UN somewhat intended. (236)

Javier Pérez de Cuéllar and the End of the Cold War (Chapter 14)

Peruvian Javier Perez de Cuellar was a famous secretary-general of the UN in the '90s. He wanted to reorient the UN mission statement to focus on peace and security, and that required reestablishing the prominence of international law.

> He concluded, "We are perilously near to a new international anarchy." The secretary-general said that his most urgent goal was to render the United Nations

capable of carrying out its primary function—collective action for peace and security. (238)

The Persian Gulf War (Chapter 15)

The Persian Gulf War was a wrong move Iraq made that provoked a unilateral and disproportionate reaction from the US, and Iraq became a victim of that war. The comportment of the US and its allies violated international law and took the UN out of its mission to maintain peace and security.

> Yet the two concepts did not exclude each other. Whether special cases or not, the Gulf War could still be a watershed. By changing the way the UN operated, the war was surely a crucial event. But the diplomacy about the war needs to be examined in some detail to make clear what it achieved for the United Nations, at least in the 1990s, and where, in fact, it sowed seeds for a nettlesome future. (255)

Boutros Boutros-Ghali (Chapters 16–19)

UN Secretary-General Boutros Boutros-Ghali, strong in character, ran the UN forcefully. The US was involved in many controversies on issues including Bosnia, Somalia, and Rwanda with Boutros-Ghali. Madeline Albright, US ambassador to the UN, accused Boutros-Ghali of trying to "arrogate more power" (285), but Boutros-Ghali, an Egyptian intellectual, did not fear the superpower.

> Boutros Boutros-Ghali startled a rare news conference in May 1994 by declaring that he might seek a second five-year term as secretary-general of the United Nations. "The question will be raised in 1996," said the seventy-one-year-old former Egyptian diplomat and law professor, "and it will depend on my physical capacities. If I feel in shape, I will say yes quite honestly. On the other hand ... if I do not feel well enough, then I will

not request a second term." Until then, he had insisted that he did not intend to stand for a second term, a stance that allowed him to wield his independence like a shield of honor. (274)

But Boutros-Ghali faced severe dilemmas concerning Bosnia, Somalia, and Rwanda. Some scholars had qualified those crises as horrors because of the huge number of casualties. By that time, Boutros-Ghali had not fully supported the US. Notwithstanding, the decision taken by Boutros-Ghali was different from the US idea. Therefore, peacekeeping missions failed because of limited human and material resources.

Murderous Hutu rioting erupted, causing thousands of Tutsi deaths. The Tutsi-dominated army put down the rebellion with enormous force, killing as many Hutus. The total slaughter of Hutus and Tutsis was somewhere between 30,000 and 100,000. Another 350,000 Hutus fled across the border into Rwanda, carrying lurid tales of Tutsi barbarity. Many of these refugees would be among the first to wield their machetes against Tutsis in Rwanda a few months later. (331)

Kofi Annan: The Accidental Secretary-General (Chapters 20–21)

Kofi Annan should not have been a secretary-general of the UN as a journalist. While this may be true, some scholars called Annan's accession to the position of secretary-general an accident because the Africans were supposed to have a representative as the Americans put pressure on Boutros-Ghali not to take an additional term. Despite that, Albright chose him as a candidate for the post of secretary-general. Annan managed the UN exceptionally well. He intervened directly to avoid some severe conflicts such as the US and Iraqi war. Sadly, at the end of his second term, his son was involved in a scandal.

Most critics took the high total of the winked-at smuggling, slapped it onto the smaller total of actual "oil for food" corruption, and came up with a whopping figure for what they called the "oil for food scandal." One of the loudest voices, Senator Norm Coleman, Republican of Minnesota, even doubled the total and came up with a $21 billion scandal. (357)

Despite that, many leaders and citizens recognized his excellent performance as secretary-general of the UN. He clarified the mission statement of the UN through his actions. He made the whole world believe in the UN. US officials appreciated Annan for his significant contribution to the UN.

He untangled relations with the United States. "I found Kofi to be one of the most skillful political animals in the world," said the American ambassador, Bill Richardson. Richard Holbrooke, who succeeded Richardson, proclaimed that Annan was the best UN secretary-general in history. (357)

Ban Ki-moon—The Slippery Eel (Chapter 22)

Ban Ki-moon replaced Kofi Annan as secretary-general of the UN; it was an Asian's time to be in that position. Ban did an excellent job for the big countries, but in the case of Haiti, Ban let the Nepalese contingent transport cholera to the country, and it killed more than ten thousand Haitians, and many others became infected because the UN did not build toilets for the peacekeepers in Haiti. That was negligence that violated international law. All soldiers should be tested for diseases before being sent abroad.

The end of the cold war reopened the door for the UN to take control of peace and security worldwide.

The end of the Cold War broke that dominance and made the UN relevant again. There were some naive hopes that it could quickly assume the policeman role envisioned by the founders, but this proved beyond its immediate reach. Well-meaning failures like the

missions to Bosnia and Somalia forced the organization
to scale down its ambitions. (379)

The UN was founded as an international entity to create and maintain peace, but it has never achieved that goal. The process for electing a UN secretary-general requires too much negotiation, compromise, and consensus. That process restricts the secretariat-general from working freely to accomplish the UN's goal of maintaining security and peace. That restriction allows the UN to fail at all times in its missions. The secretariat-general position has become a political domination job because the permanent members want access to it.

Nonetheless, the five permanent members of the UN contributed to that failure because they had a scary plan to destroy the world for their particular interests. The whole history of the UN shows that the secretariat-general position is a political game, and the responsibility is a headache that involves dilemmas, deception, and misery despite its privileges.

The Failure of the United Nations

The P5 comprises the permanent members of the Security Council, and the E10 is the group of nonpermanent members. How did the P5 and the E10 become two different entities in the UN's Security Council? International relations is a field of political science that studies international relations. It also determines the relations and interaction between international personalities and sovereign states in terms of their cooperation, commerce, and diplomacy. The UN comprises 193 members. Each of them has a mandate of two years, not renewable but rotatable in an internal election held by the General Assembly. Thus, both groups are enslaved by socioeconomic gaps.

It is a crucial problem for the UN because a significant gap has handicapped the P5 and the E10. Those two groups developed a relationship between global north and global south. The P5 controls the organization socially, culturally, economically, and politically with its veto status. The E10 is a negligible entity almost entirely in the Security Council, which is the decision-making organ of the UN. In that matter, the UN has become almost dysfunctional and fails to achieve its goal of promoting peace and security in the world.

The P5 Is Hegemonic in the UN

The P5 contributes a huge sum of the money that finances UN missions to resolve conflicts. The capacities and capabilities of the P5 to construct some unstable social, economic, and political systems make it a dominating and imposing structure in the UN; all decisions must have their agreement before they can be applied. Sometimes, the powerful countries create personal conflicts to evoke humanitarian missions that so-called human-made catastrophes to intervene without durable solutions in the global south countries. Some scholars mention that the P5 was deconstructed to gain profits or to force developing countries to negotiate essential deals.

Some catastrophes are caused by Mother Nature, and the P5 has significant infrastructure and some reliable social structures that cover and monitor their citizens' positive and negative rights including trade in goods, services, and exchanges with low taxation. Therefore, employment is low, and its citizens refuse to perform some kinds of work. Thus, they can assist the immigrants with work visas or change their status so the strangers have to refuse citizens' jobs. The tax the immigrants pay strengthens the economy and generates luxury for the P5 countries that make the tourism industry accumulate financial resources. That is right; the P5 remains the dominant country group.

The P5 manipulates the UN and violates some treaties and conventions in time and space to act unilaterally for its interests, for instance, the US and Iraq war, USSR and Crimea, the UK, and Argentina.

> When Germany assumed its seat in January 2003, one would have been hard-pressed to predict how much relations with the United States would sour over the next couple of years over the U.S. decision to invade Iraq without Council support. (Romita, Fink, and Papenfuss 2011)

Customization of the UN Rules Violation by the P5

Those kinds of irresponsible rhetorical attitudes tarnish the UN's reputation and integrity, but such violations have a long history of about seventy years.

> The P 5 have been the dominant UNSC force for the last 70 years. This has been a key factor in maintaining a concert of interest among the most powerful nations. (Langmore and Thakur 103)

Some observers argue that the UNSC is not a democratic organ of the UN; for that reason, they want to bring its treaties, conventions, and resolutions into question.

The E10 is elected but neglected, Langmore and Thakur said. It is a negligible component of the UNSC. The E10 members do not have veto rights. In some cases, the P5 employs soft or hard diplomacy to make the E10 vote in favor of or against certain projects. Some scholars argue that the E10 is mistreated because the P5 countries have a significant GDPs, vast economic affairs, military power, and stable governmental institutions. At the same time, the E10 is supported financially by the P5. Like the ancient adage, "Who finances commands." Therefore, the superpower states employ strategies to coerce and corrupt the most impoverished states. The E10 encompasses eminent social crucial obstacles in terms of positive and negative rights, which become a global calamity. Certain countries have different rank levels compared to others. Among the E10, some are developing countries, some are underdeveloped countries, and some are so-called Third World countries. Countries with fewer assets could be easily corrupted by a member of the P5. At that point, they become vulnerable, weak, and inoperative in the Security Council.

The E10 Barriers

The E10 has some fundamental barriers that cause its negative performance in the UNSC; the barriers include social, economic, and political factors. Those factors generate conflicts of superiority and inferiority between the E10 and the P5. Therefore, a modus operandi and a modus vivendi are required to fill the gap.

> At least at the rhetorical level, the reality of global inequality and Third World poverty is a pressing issue. For instance, the official institutions of Bretton Woods post–World War II liberalism. (Kacowicz 2)

The lack of basic resources such as food, water, sanitation, and housing constitutes a significant source of poverty that the E10 cannot solve. Furthermore, the economic barriers emphasize the basic infrastructure like transportation, communication, electrification, and industrialization. The lack of those systems facilitates the absence of employment that keeps citizens in poverty. Those barriers cause the E10 to be neglected by the P5. The political factor is the primary key that the P5 applies to keep the E10 population in misery and exploit E10's resources both natural and human. Despite this fact, the elections become a farce and tricky to impose corrupt candidates, drug dealers, bandits, and kidnappers and select them to rule the country. For instance, in Haiti, Hilary Clinton as secretary of state imposed on Michael Martelly, a kidnapper, drug dealer, and a bandit legally but well known to be president in exchange for giving her brother a monopoly on the gold mine in the country. As a result, famine, gang proliferation, and emigration are everywhere globally—for example, the mass of Haitian refugees in Del Rio, Texas.

Effectiveness and Legitimacy of the E10

The E10 is a significant component of the UNSC that exercises or rules chapters 6 and 7 of the UN charter to order and monitor the protection and deployment of military missions in case of intra- or intercountry conflicts, but it cannot make influential contributions to UNSC decisions whether social, economic, or political because its members' terms of election are limited to two years. If the E10 tries to influence a decision in the UNSC, any of the P5 can veto it.

E10 members can nevertheless make influential contributions to the Security Council's decision making processes during their two-year Council term. (Langmore and Farrall 93)

However, the E10 gives legitimacy to the UNSC. The UN is legitimate because of the presence of the E10 as a component of the P5 that makes the UNSC an entity. The E10 must be treated equally with the P5 in terms of the legal organ of the UNSC. Otherwise, structural reform has to change the status of the UNSC as some observers propose. Whether to add more permanent and elected members to the Security Council is an issue; some or all of the prerogatives of the P5 such as veto rights and nuclear rights should be abolished.

The Security Council gains much of its legitimacy from the election of ten of its members by a two-thirds majority of member states. The E10 serves two-year terms, five being elected each year. (Langmore and Thakur 106)

The UN is composed of three eminent structures: the Security Council, the General Assembly (GA), and the General Secretariat, headed by the secretary-general. The UNSC itself is divided into the P5, the dominant group, and the E10, the neglected group. The GA comprises the state members including the P5 and E10 members. The secretary-general is the chief executive of the UN. The E10 plays a fundamental role in UNSC.

This year, the simultaneous tenures of several powerful developing countries among the E10 on the Security Council could help assure the broader membership that the discourse on international counterterrorism efforts will take their varied views into greater account. (Romita et al. 2011)

In Contrast

Some scholars argue that the UN creates a better world by solving conflicts of all sorts, but it has exacerbated more disputes than before. The UN is an undemocratic entity because the process that created it was unfair; the permanent members had veto rights over UN resolutions and who became members of the E10.

The UN needs to be reformed because there are more independent states, which the P5 might try to strip of their resources. Nowadays, the UN looks like an evil and corrupt organization that encourages gangsters instead of protecting people. For instance, the BINUH in Haiti acclaims the crimes perpetrated by gangs on civil society and submits a report to the secretary-general to read in the UNSC. It is a crime that the UN associates itself with state crimes.

The P5 Reveals a Stagnant Obstacle for Merging with the E10

The P5 utilizes its technology and capital to establish itself globally by hiring cheap labor to produce goods. Often, those workers work overtime and do not have enough time to rest and eat properly. What they produce allows corporations to expand the market for their products all over the world. The products are not sent for free to the periphery country people.

> The core countries make rules of international trade, often by direct political control of the periphery. (Shiraev and Zubok 89)

> In the resulting world economy, resources are underpriced; there is overproduction by one country and over-consumption by the other. These results have been extended to a dynamic context in Chichilnisky (1993c). (Chichilnisky 3)

The elite economies play the role of international agents to become rich instead of advocating to change the working conditions, wages, and the price of commodities to boost the GDP of global south countries and boost their people above the poverty line.

> Local elites in the periphery also are interested in this economic order because they pocket most profits from selling natural resources of their countries to the core countries. (Choen 89)

Marxists have good reason to identify capitalism as an asymmetric financial system that creates two poles of the economy and divides the world into a global north and a global south that needs financial restructuring to liberate the markets and democratize the economic system. It infers that the significant gap within those two variables in the domain of international relations, the P5 and the E10, makes it very difficult for the UN to promote security and peace in the world. Decision-making is asymmetric and in favor of the P5; that attitude tarnishes the UN's reputation.

International Institutions

Treaties, conventions, and international laws connect sovereign countries in the cadre of cooperation in multiple domains. The UN agencies call the treaties to regulate some political, socioeconomic, and cultural paradigms to monitor and defend people's rights. The treaties must apply equally to all sovereign countries that ratify them.

The review of UN membership for Haiti is the sine qua non because the treaties are wrongly and inequitably applied to southern countries or impoverished countries. That is unfair because all members pay their dues, and the UN must fix that abnormality and especially in the case of the Vienna Treaty.

Vienna Treaty

The Vienna Treaty established and defined the friendship between sovereign countries, which exchange ambassadors. The norm of the Vienna Treaty is that each country has an ambassador as its representative, not multiple ambassadors. The Core Group has not existed in the Vienna Treaty, group ambassador friends of a country who are accredited in the country that decides behalf of a sovereign country. It is a systematic violation of the Vienna Treaty in the case of Haiti, a sovereign country. To demode Haiti as the first black country independent in the world that requests an entire battle, that country must be victorious and proclaim that the hegemonic state defeats Haiti and that Haiti is no longer an independent state anymore; it is a colony. Otherwise, violating the treaties to reduce a nation as a "shithole" is not a pleasant journey.

Haiti Is Too Close to the US

Haiti is too close to the US, which has diplomatic relations between countries that refer to similar cooperation, ratification of protocol exchange, services, trade, peace agreements, and many other types of cooperation. In terms of cooperation controlled by the Vienna Treaty, international relations require a deep respect for the customary laws that monitor those international relations. Nonetheless, developed countries frequently violate the principle of respecting undeveloped countries. The US, which dictates to the other members of the Core Group, utilizes its power to destabilize the state structure in Haiti because it has a robust economy, a military network, and power over granting visas that they can revoke to pressure citizens to keep silent about violations of customary and domestic laws.

The US is too close to Haiti to humiliate the country like that. The Core Group and the US organize false elections and select whom they want to become president, members of Congress, chief of police, and others. The Core Group selects officials illegally to destroy the institutions of the country, which are the backbone of the state.

The US accepted sacrificing Haiti by violating the Vienna Treaty that established the rules of diplomacy. The Vienna Treaty determines how international persons establish international relations between sovereign states that accredit their ambassadors. However, how the occidental countries apply the treaty to impoverished countries systematically violates the mission statement regulating the nation-states' relationships.

States that violate international laws remain unpunished by the UN secretary-general.

It is unlawful for a group of ambassadors to replace the national officials to run a country in the wrong direction. It is inconceivable that the UN spent millions of dollars and more than fifteen years stabilizing the country by sending different missions such as MINUSTAH, MINUAH, and BUNUH. Those missions created more instability and increased criminality in Haiti.

The UN claims that the G9 was founded and federated to reduce the number of killings and kidnappings for ransom. People do not have that amount of money, and the victims of kidnappings are sometimes abused before their captors received the ransom, which the kidnappers at times demand two or three times, a heavy burden for the many Haitians who struggle financially.

State Official's Involvement

When kidnappings started in 2004, the public considered them to be crimes prompted by politics. Some state officials were involved in kidnappings with the help of gang members who had access to police resources such as uniforms, arms, and vehicles. Members of gangs establish supremacy over faithful police officers, and they pose as traffic agents, law enforcement officials, and judges, but the government ignores that unlawful behavior. Those criminals operate without fear of the law and citizens because they work primarily for the government.

State's Responsibility

The state is responsible for protecting the lives and property of its citizens, and that requires a reliable national security system. Impunity has to be banned, and the justice department has to be active. The systematic control of guns must be strict with no exceptions either for hegemonic states or nationals, who receive guns and distribute them to the gangs.

Nonetheless, the carelessness of the state puts the population in a profound dilemma of fear. The stratagem of the bandits pushes people to flee their homes and find refuge elsewhere, but that makes their health more vulnerable to disease.

National Properties

All lands containing resources such as gold, silver, bronze, oil, uranium, and others are national properties. Gold is the main mineral resource that interests hegemonic states and the agencies that work for them. Gold is extracted from rivers, mountains, forests, and agrarian lands, but peasants who forage for gold can degrade the environment and put themselves at the risk of death.

Democracy—A Model of the Trinity

The global north imposed a democratic model of the Trinity. The Bible is the ideological basis of the capitalist system that contains the spiritual policy. The objective of the Bible is to dominate believers and make them submit to all sorts of social conditions. The occidental countries created a prototype democracy while they connected the theorem of Montesquieu, which is the balance and division of state building. That formula is to connect Jesus Christ, the Holy Spirit, and God with governments composed of a parliament, a judiciary, and an executive branch. Jesus Christ is similar to the legislative branch, the Holy Spirit is similar to the judiciary branch, and God is similar to the executive branch.

Jesus Christ preached a policy of the divine kingdom and modified the laws of the Old Testament. He promised to return for those who believed in him. The Holy Spirit protects believers from calamity, God saves believers from Satan with his advice and intervention, and Jesus Christ plays the role of advocate and lawyer for the salvation of believers. The capitalist system established the Trinity formula to keep the poor people poorer.

Repartimiento

Developing countries use the concept of repartimiento to refer to their requests for a fair redistribution of national resources and for their inclusion in public institutions. In most cases, some individuals characterize themselves as a super race, a dominant majority that excludes others from benefitting from countries' wealth.

The need for repartimiento is necessary for Haiti; equal redistribution of its goods and services must start now. Haiti's wealth is controlled by a heterogeneous bourgeoise from different countries in the Middle East. Occidental countries want to exterminate the first independent black nation, and they work for its failure. State properties were transferred to the private sector. That sector closed national industries such as Teleco, a communication company, Cement d'Haiti, Acierie d'Haiti, an iron company, and Hasco, a sugar company.

The products these companies had produced had to then be imported, and the products were of an inferior quality. They forced the population to buy them in spite of the fact that the privatization of those industries created monstrous unemployment.

Food production in Haiti almost disappeared because its production was insufficient to feed the whole population. The Food and Agriculture Organization (FAO) predicts that 4.5 million people will be subject to famine. Land that was once used to raise crops was given to people who wanted to plant other crops for the benefit of multinationals. Ten thousand hectares were taken from peasants and given to an individual for criminal purposes.

A process to calculate the country's assets that should be redistributed is critical. Land should be remitted to peasants, and tax money must finance public institutions such as schools and hospitals. The state has to monitor and build infrastructure including roads, communication systems, electricity, bridges, transportation, and technology. Haitians deserve a better life, and an accurate repartimiento can to that.

Nonrepartimiento Consequences

Haiti is dominated by a syndicate of diplomats, the so-called Core Group consisting of ambassadors from occidental countries wanting Haiti without the Haitians. It wants to seize Haitian resources regardless of the reais, conventions, and bilateral and multilateral agreements. That is called stealing even though they are considered hegemonic states.

The US is at the head of that evil project, which is based on racism, prejudice, and hate of those with dark skin. That situation gives birth to a vast immigration movement all over the place and especially to the United States. Dramatically, US immigration has sent Haitians back to their country even though international law protects them. The refugees returned to Haiti without knowing their status; they were just sent back to Haiti to be killed by gangsters. There are no natural, academic, or constitutional norms that authorize a powerful state to humiliate, abuse, and exterminate those who come from a sovereign state because of the color of their skin. Europeans and Americans must stop that nasty attitude.

The US considers Haitians to be its enemy though nobody, not even the government, admits that. But the US occupied Haiti two times for no reason, took the gold crown, and killed many citizens. The Americans came to the country to arrest President Jean Bertrand Aristide on February 29, 2004. The US also fomented several coups d'état to destabilize the country's economy; that increased unemployment, and it allowed those they put in power to commit financial crimes. Those acts demonstrated how the US hates Haiti due to its desire for its natural resources and the skin color of its citizens and even for its great history, some critics say.

Haitians have to realize that Americans do not want to be their friends; they prefer to be their enemies for the reasons cited above. Haitians must consider them as the enemy and gradually reduce their relationship with them. All sovereign countries are interconnected based on their international needs. If one country cannot deal with another, it should leave that country alone and break off diplomatic relations. No country should abuse another based on racist ideology.

The concept of repartimiento also applies in the field of international affairs. On this point, the US is called out by some critics for various acts of sabotage and illegal seizure of Haitian assets. The US has to remit the properties that still belong to Haiti including the gold crown, the land that the US occupies illegally, for instance, the island of La Navase, and the money donated for earthquake relief in 2010 that was taken by American foundations including the American Red Cross. The amount, up to $20 billion, cannot reconstruct Haiti, but it can ameliorate several social issues. The most important thing is that the US must back off from Haiti for the country's well-being.

All Haitians must demand the repartimiento of the country's assets, and they can do so with the support of groups, organizations, and institutions. Haitians must organize massive marches, sit-ins, and large movements of solidarity to mobilize the world for Haiti to get back the money and the properties from ancient colonizers to reconstruct a new state because the occidental countries and their organizations are trying to destroy Haiti as an international personality.

CHAPTER 7

$$\infty$$

H_2O

Water is essential for life. In Haiti, rivers are a main source of water; Haitians use that water to drink, cook, bathe, wash clothes, electric barrage, and irrigate crops.

In rural Haiti, however, water that has been purified by nature is polluted by corporations that misuse the water for their own benefit such as mining, and the water becomes contaminated by chemical products. Corporations capture water sources so they can purify it and sell it in bottles, and that can make water a luxury for impoverished people.

Corporations also privatize water to be used in alternative drinks like Coca-Cola, Pepsi, and other soft drinks. These corporations include Nestle, Sysco, JBS, George Weston, Tyson Foods, Bunge, Pepsico, and Mondelez. The food industry uses vast amounts of water to grow the crops that the agroindustry uses including sugar cane for those beverages and for many other food products. The quantity of water available in particular regions of the globe has been reduced considerably because companies like Coca-Cola and Pepsi buy fertile lands that contain water to cultivate the coca plant. This is the case in Mexico.

As a result, many people end up drinking Coke instead of water because it is cheaper than a bottle of water. That reality is expected to affect emerging countries; some predict that state water will be challenging to find. Consequently, the middle class, the proletariat, cannot afford to buy a cup of water. In the end, that product has to be protected to prevent people from dying of thirst. The authorities protect those food industries, and some authorities are shareholders; that is why regulation fails.

Those in Haiti who forage in the rivers for gold release chemicals used in that process into the rivers, which poisons water there and thus in other drinking water sources. Such foraging is a disaster for the creatures that live in the water and on which many depend as a source of food.

Contaminated Water

Contaminated water usually contains microbes and bacteria that are harmful to people and can cause fever, diarrhea, and other diseases. Cholera, a virus found in contaminated water, can sicken and kill many people who come in contact with it, and that can cause cholera epidemics, endemics, and pandemics.

Generally speaking, viruses and bacteria can both cause disease. However, the difference between them is that viruses cannot reproduce without a host whereas bacteria can reproduce without a host. The cholera virus is an old pathogen. According to Sonia Shah, the cholera virus outbreak in the 1830s spread worldwide as it was supported by contaminated by fecal matter and neglect of personal hygiene such as handwashing.

> The cure for cholera is clean water, plus a smattering of simple electrolytes like salts. This elementary treatment reduces cholera mortality from 50 percent to less than 1 percent. (Shah 142)

The last outbreak of cholera in Haiti came after the earthquake in January 2010. When the UN sent a contingent of Nepalese soldiers without medical tests, the soldiers introduced cholera into the country. Some observers thought that that was negligence or an attempt to kill Haitians because the UN refused to compensate the victims of cholera. Since then, cholera has become an endemic disease in Haiti and continues to kill people. Nowadays, cholera can be cured, but better private and public sanitation and hygiene can stop its spread.

Medecin finally figured out how to cure cholera. It just hadn't done so fast enough to deliver humanity from nearly a century of cholera pandemics. (Shah 231)

Our planet has a vast amount of natural water, enough for all purposes. People and animals can drink in quality and quantity without exploitation and prejudice between northern and southern countries.

Disasters Are a Source of Fraud and Discrimination

Some countries face natural and human-made disasters because some people create disasters to generate money. Think of firefighters that might be tempted to start fires to have something to do. That can cost losses of life and property.

Some community activists consider disasters as sources of profits to earn money from the victims. In the US, the federal government gives money distributed to local, regional, and federal agencies, and the money is budgeted to help those in need. However, the money requested is more than what is needed to cover the expenditures for the catastrophic incident, which means more money stays in the organizers' hands. It has become a habit for local and regional leaders to get money from deadly calamities. Equally important, wildfires, tornados, and floods hit some areas regularly, and those areas have a permanent rescue staff to help victims. That means that they have a permanent budget and that fraudsters have a permanent source of revenue.

Discrimination

Some fraudulent organizers serve people of color differently than they do white people while all people suffer from the same dilemma. When a tornado hits, for instance, they can distribute their aid asymmetrically; they can serve white victims first, and black people get whatever is left over. White supremacists exclude minorities from public affairs, public offices, and public wealth, and they are ready to utilize violence to keep out minorities and especially black people. They divide the minority into four categories to control their access to what they are entitled to and to marginalize them.

61

Haiti's Catastrophes

Haiti is a country of catastrophes due to hurricanes, earthquakes, and rain that affect its people in many ways and keep them below the poverty line. Actors collect goods that are supposed to be shared with the vulnerable people, but officials and others profit at the expense of the victims of these tragedies.

Hurricanes constitute a significant threat to the country; the hurricane season starts in June and ends in November, and the beginning of that season raises the fears of the vulnerable, who think they might lose all they have, become homeless, and require medication and emergency services. In contrast, national and international agencies welcome that season because they can amass money and sell supplies to the needy people.

The hurricane season mobilizes many NGOs in Haiti to seek money, but they do not have good coordination; they either don't know the country or are not qualified to try to help it or do a mediocre job of distributing money and supplies. They work in the same field and stay in the same area to do the same things while communities have different needs and emergencies such as the lack of water, food, shelter, and medical assistance. The minister does not have a proper policy for canalizing the NGOs to deliver humanitarian assistance where it is most needed.

Further, the minister does not have a plan for the whole country in diverse fields including reconstruction, repairs, and credit plans to help victims overcome their misery and relaunch their financial activities. Haiti does not have an agroindustry system, thus no avocados, mangos, plantains, or oranges. Hurricanes can topple trees onto houses and streets, and rain can create massive flooding that can wash crops and even animals away. In August 1980, Hurricane David did exactly that and caused food prices including meat to soar incredibly because of high demand and a lack of supply.

Hurricanes render Haiti vulnerable and miserable, but state officials are blind to that and are too corrupt; they do not build infrastructure to protect the country and the population from disasters human-made and natural.

Earthquakes in Haiti range from magnitude 4 to magnitude 7.2 on the Richter scale. An earthquake in January 2010 killed and injured many, and a number of people were simply never heard from again. According to Claude Preptit, a Haitian geologist and director of the Bureau of Mines in Haiti, the country has several tectonic plates that gain energy that can cause severe earthquakes. Haitians are still waiting for that catastrophe that has not happened yet. However, the Haitians saw their country destroyed, their families killed, the cost of living shoot up, and the rate of poverty increase.

Some critics say that some earthquakes are caused by the hegemonic state that wants to steal Haiti's gas. Earthquakes are frequent in Haiti and especially in two regions—Grand-Danse and Nippes—where 7.2 magnitude earthquakes hit, but some argue that earthquakes in those areas are abnormal. Many aftershocks continued to shake up those regions. While this may be true, another country could export gas to another country without authorization, contract, and benefit. The United Nations Convention on the Law of the Sea limits the ability of countries to violate the international territorial boundaries of other countries, but superpowers can take by force the belongings of less-powerful countries such as Haiti. It is unacceptable for a sovereign country to impose authoritarian personnel on another country to seize its assets.

The north countries, especially the US, have antidemocratic policies toward Haiti to capture its properties; that is unlawful and an abuse of power because Haiti does not have a propositional force of frappe compared to that of the United States.

Inhabitants of Grand-Anse reported that they saw some boats, helicopters, and divers in the sea. They asked the Haitian fishermen to leave the sea areas, and they accompanied them back to the shore. The residents heard and felt some explosions and aftershocks after that. People thought that it was an undersea exploitation of free gas.

While the US policy is to send Haitian refugees back to Haiti, it welcomes white refugees, for instance, Ukrainians, and has assistance ready to give to them because they are Whites. The US government cannot intervene there and try to seize Ukrainian assets, but in the case of Haitians, police officers in the US use slavery practices to humiliate them in public; the mistreatment was reported on national TV. Moreover, the US government deported Haitians while gangs controlled the country under the supervision of the UN, which conducted several peacekeeping missions over a fifteen-year period. Instead of securing the country, they let Haiti became a forum for criminals established by Madam La Lime and Antonio Gutierrez.

The US hates Haitians, but people should not be repatriated to any country with a high level of crime and religious and political persecution. The US returned them without examining their claims to asylum, and the US needs free stuff from Haitians. It is not fair.

In response to the 2010 earthquake in Haiti, several countries, stars in different disciplines, and other individuals donated money to support the victims and the reconstruction of the country. The American Red Cross kept around $20 million of that. The French government made Haiti pay around $17 billion for its independence, and the Clinton foundation had several other million to reconstruct Haiti. The truth is that Haiti was never reconstructed. Dominican companies have several million-dollar contracts to build public offices and roads. One day, those amounts must return to the Haitian people.

What Is Your Zip Code?

Your zip code indicates where you live in the US. In Chicago, if your zip code is in the South and West sides, you are faced with discrimination, neglect, and insufficient assistance. The red color on the map symbolizes black or minority areas.

Zip codes are hints of people's economic status; people in certain zip codes tend to be poor and lacking in necessities while people in certain other zip codes are wealthier and enjoy excellent schools, hospitals, firefighters, expensive stores, restaurants, parks, good infrastructure, and security and safety. Zip codes are indications of the status, ethnicity, and skin color of those who live in them. For instance, zip code 60043, Kenilworth, Illinois, has the most billionaires while zip code 62523, Decatur, Illinois, has the poorest people.

Kenilworth

Kenilworth is the wealthiest suburb in Cook County, Illinois, with a population of 2,512 and 4,128, which refers to the density of the population. The median age there is forty-four, the median home value is over $1,000,000, the median rent is $4,931, and schools there rate from 7 to 10 on a 10-point scale. The per capita income there is $105,512, and the crime index is 39, typical for a prosperous community. Only 6 percent of people there rent their homes or apartments, and the median property tax is $10,000. Kenilworth is 89 percent white, 3 percent Asian, and 8 percent other races; Blacks are not noted separately.

Prejudice and Economic Status

Prejudice is based on skin color. Blacks cannot integrate into white communities; that excludes them from the opportunity that the dominant class takes all for itself. Empirical evidence shows the negative aspect of politics on minority economic development in the US. Those economic factors can never help minorities and particularly black entrepreneurs overcome poverty and receive funds for their own businesses.

> The Florida legislature created the Florida black business Investment Board to support the creation and expansion of the black-owned business. Specifically, the board was charged with increasing employment opportunities, strengthening the state's economy, and increasing the number of Black business enterprises. (Florida Black Business Investment Board 1994)

It is not an easy task for members of minority groups to raise the money their members need to fund their own businesses. The dominant white group is anti-immigration; it refuses to share opportunities with multiethnic groups. While they decide to do so, they make confident choices. The first choice is Asian ethnic groups; the second is Hispanic groups; the third choice is Caribbean ethnic groups, and the last choice is native-born African Americans. The dominant group leaves a tight margin for black minority entrepreneurs to succeed.

Some black people cannot afford to live in wealthy areas. They are excluded from having an equal part of the wealth of this country, which spreads to neighborhoods where the dominant class lives. Socially, white people use discrimination to humiliate black people with the stereotype of the enslaved as the enslaver. The dominant class treats Blacks as an inferior class and accuses them of all sorts of crimes including felonies, misdemeanors, inchoate offenses, and strict liability offenses. When members of the dominant class commit crimes, the judicial system gives them light punishment if it even charges them at all. Blacks can be falsely charged for crimes and sent to jail for many years or even life. Black people cannot live in Kenilworth for racist reasons.

Blacks must organize civil rights movements to gain opportunities for advancement. Some pessimistic elements set up barriers to keep minorities from growing economically. All colored ethnic groups have some access to financial resources even if they are not lawfully and equally distributed; some groups receive more resources than others do. The black minority is at the lower end of those receiving resources and simple admission to public affairs. Indeed, to put themselves in the magical instrumental society, collective actions and lawsuits are required.

> Scholars of black politics rightly argue that black political empowerment has not to date resulted in social and economic equality. (Watson 1994)

The lower class, black people, does not have the right to negotiate loans; they have a preference in choosing the amount. The first-come first-served policy does not apply to them. Black entrepreneurs have been constrained to taking the leftovers.

Economic Status

The dominant class's white privilege creates socially constructed barriers to keep Blacks in extreme poverty. Black people have financial barriers that prevent them from getting loans, and the high-paying jobs are reserved for white people even when black people are more qualified than their white counterparts. Whites are paid more than Blacks even when they do the same work. Therefore, black people can never afford to even rent a house in Kenilworth.

Regarding Education in Kenilworth

Master's Degree is 48%, Bachelor's Degree is 44%. Some college or associate's Degrees are 4 %; High School diplomas or Equivalent 1%, and the unemployment rate is 5%. Healthcare is 6%, finance is 27%, less than $10000 is 5%, and more than 200000 is 59%. (nextburb.com)

Decatur is the poorest city in Illinois. The poverty line is 32.1 %, overall poverty is 16.6%, neighborhoods with concentrated poverty 6 out of 34, and the jobless rate in poor neighborhoods is 19.8%. Source: 24/7 Wall St. (centersquare.com)

In Decatur, the median home price is $77,300, and the median rent is $851. The property tax is $1,974. The schools rate 1 to 7 on a 10-point scale. Its population is 71,857, population density is 1,724, and the median age is forty. Decatur's population is 70 percent white, 3 percent Asian, and 23 percent black; two other races make up 5 percent and 1 percent of its populace.

Regarding Education in Decatur

In Decatur, 8 percent have a master's degree, 14 percent have a bachelor's degree, 32 percent have some college experience or an associate's degree, 36 percent have high school diploma or the equivalent, and 10 percent have less than a high school diploma.

Financial Status

The median household income in Decatur is $45,404, the unemployment rate is 9 percent, the poverty rate is 19 percent, and income per capita is $27,813.

Ten percent of households in Decatur have incomes of less than

$10,000, and 3 percent have incomes greater than $200,000. Crime rates are elevated at 126 percent, average for a poor city with a concentrated population.

Extreme Poverty and Humiliation in Poor Zip Codes

The city's project is a wrongdoing factor that creates a poor zip code zone. Public housing usually has insufficient windows and limited space, and many cannot afford air conditioning. Streets, garbage collection, and other services can be neglected. People live in humiliating circumstances; corner stores are usually few and far between.

The absence of big stores in black neighborhoods suggests that developers ignore the development of minority communities. In black neighborhoods, many small stores belong to other ethnic groups such as Asians and Hispanics. Banks and government agencies will give them financial credits, loans, and grants to open businesses, but they do not support black business owners who want to invest in their neighborhoods. Asian and Hispanic business owners do not invest in the black communities, where they accumulate profit. They leave the environment dirty and undeveloped with no employment or social services.

Black business owners who want loans to start a business are turned down 80 percent of the time; in some cases, that is due to their low level of education. Black business owners must have excellent credit scores—no bankruptcies or civil judgments against them. Banks stand in the way of black entrepreneurs who want to start or relaunch a business by not giving them loans.

Criminal Records

Criminal records are an additional dilemma for Blacks who want to participate in some public financial programs and apply for some jobs. Convictions hold them back; white supremacy sets them up to go to prison for nonsensical matters. For instance, if they steal candy at a convenience store, they get arrested and have a police report that goes on their record. People who smoke or sell marijuana in the streets, fight at school, or engage in domestic violence can be disqualified from receiving financial assistance.

Tribulation and Contribution of Minority-Owned Businesses in the United States

Native Americans control the economy more than African Americans do. The tribulation of some minority-owned businesses is infernal, and some minority-owned businesses contribute to the US economy. Minorities are found in each country whether it is rich or poor. Most of the time, the elite find political, economic, social, and cultural ways to help minorities access national resources because of the contributions they can make to the country. But that is not the case in the US because discrimination is too common in its society.

Katherine Spilde and Jonathan B. Taylor wrote the article "The Indian Gaming Regulatory Act and Its Effects on American Indian Economic Development." That article could be titled "Indian Favoritism in the United States." The Indian minority group has most of the resources distributed; other minorities such as Blacks are banned from having even a fraction of those resources. Moreover, believe it or not, Native Americans requested fiscal independence in the US. Guess what? They got it.

Native American Economic Backgrounds

The history of Native Americans in the US is tragic. Current Native Americans live under the poverty line, their life expectancy is lower than average, and their desires are inadequate. The prospect for their future is uncertain; they will live under the poverty line.

> A number of obstacles to effective political rule and economic development help explain the persistence of reservation poverty. (Spilde 6)

Native Americans were the first to inhabit some parts of what is now the US. Native American tribes gained fiscal independence by negotiation, treaties, and executive orders: "Most American Indian reservations were established by treaties and executive orders in the 19th century" (5). In contrast, other parts of the US including Louisiana,

California, Arizona, and New Mexico were added by conquest or purchase.

Meanwhile, Native Americans claim the land on which they lived based on their tradition, religion, belief, and living styles.

> By the late 1960s and early 1970s, American Indian assertions of tribal sovereignty via litigation and political action heralded the contemporary "Self-Determination Era," The federal government delegated powers and responsibilities to tribal governments. This era provided greater autonomy to tribal governments in the determination of their political institutions, economic activities, and development (Wilkins 2002). (Spilde 5)

Because of their fiscal independence, Native Americans were able to establish their financial activities, which focus on gaming.

Gaming Benefits and Affirmative Action Programs

Income from casinos gives Native Americans the capital they need to invest in their reservations. With fiscal independence, the tribes' lifestyles changed; they had the money needed to benefit low-income people and construct schools, parks, hospitals, elderly centers, recreation centers, and many more lucrative and nonlucrative facilities for the benefit of their citizens. They invested in casinos, motels, hotels, markets, and grocery stores. They do not pay taxes, but they are authorized to make some contributions.

> In many cases, tribes have invested in nearby retail businesses, outlet malls, and other businesses that take advantage of customer traffic. Finally, they turn toward more distinct sectors as varied as banking (Citizen Potawatomi Nation), commercial real estate (San Manuel), and federal facilities management (Winnebago), often redeploying the management experience gained in tribal gaming development. The operation of tribal gaming facilities has also changed

labor markets on reservations. Opening tribal gaming facilities increases the demand for both high-and low-skill laborers on the reservation. New employment opportunities exist in management and professional positions in the gaming and tourism industries. (Spilde 197)

Tribal governments use gaming cash to create jobs, invest in infrastructure, and gain access to financial capital while black communities are discriminated against based on skin color.

Tourism Expenditures

Tourism is another source of income for Native Americans. Facilities such as casinos, hotels, motels, and grocery stores generate profits more quickly than do facilities in other economic fields because tourists tend to spend their money on amenities in hotels and casinos, and casinos alone employ more than 20,000 non-Native Americans.

Survey data from Washington State tribes, for example, indicate that two-thirds of the 27,376 workers employed in tribal casinos, governments, and non-gaming enterprises in 2010 were non-Indians. (Taylor 2012)

Tourism combined with luxurious accommodations generates a significant amount of money for tribal governments.

Tribal governments have also used the revenues from gaming to fund other economic development, based on the widely shared view that Indian gaming will not provide sustained economic growth indefinitely. (197)

Citizen Benefits from the Gaming Regulatory Act

Tribal communities use gaming money like a welfare system in that everybody benefits from jobs or cash. Meanwhile, people have an economy that decentralizes the reservation economically because the reservation resource is used correctly and lifts people above the poverty line.

> The amounts distributed may vary according to the revenue in a given year. The total amount of payments is not typically disclosed publicly; however, several tribal governments announce the size of their payments, which range from a few hundred to thousands of dollars per person annually. (198)

Information comes from different fields. Methodically, that information is accumulated and synchronized to educate people. Here are some of them: the US Census Bureau, surveys, individual interviews, business agencies, scholarly journal articles, the National Indian Gaming Commission, the Senate Commission on Indian Affairs, and the Harvard Project on American Indian Economic Development. These entities contribute to making the literature available to the public.

The author of this article wants readers to see the substantial spectrum of the fissure between minorities. To this extent, the exclusion is not only about skin color but also about financial prejudice, which favors one racial-ethnic group over another. There are some particularities in racial backgrounds. Of course, all human beings have the same desire to live above the poverty line. Some needs might be more basic than others, but ultimately, we are all the same.

All minority groups should negotiate fiscal independence as Native American tribes have to bring prosperity to their communities by creating jobs and helping their communities with social, economic, cultural, and political support and participation. It is nonsense for an ethnic group to have a sizable financial consensus while other groups are excluded from that.

Generally, Blacks live under the lie of black capitalism. In that matter, black-owned businesses struggle to survive in their communities while Native Americans' businesses vastly contribute to their communities and thus can preserve their values, beliefs, traditions, and communities.

Social and Political Factors Impacting the Economic Status of Various Racial and Ethnic Groups in the US

Minority ethnic groups in the US confront multiple obstacles to building up their economic, social, political, and cultural lives. Those factors are linked to prejudice directed at denying immigrants opportunities to achieve entrepreneurial success. With professors Robb and Fairlie, we will do an empirical analysis starting with the backgrounds of minorities to the reasons for their economic failure. Therefore, we will compare Whites as the top within minorities and Blacks as the lowest category within owned businesses' wealth.

Multiethnic Minority-Owned Businesses in the United States

All ethnic groups come to America with a dream of prospering economically and educationally. In terms of ethnicity, some nationalities are competing to realize that dream. Asian, Hispanic, European, African, Caribbean, and Middle Eastern people are coming to the US to establish themselves and enjoy a higher standard of living. They are willing to gain education so they can work for better pay in companies or start their own businesses.

> Self-employed business owners are also unique in that they create jobs for themselves. Business ownership is the main alternative to wage/salary employment for making a living and thus has important implications for earnings and wealth inequality. Both black and white entrepreneurs are found to have more upward mobility and less downward mobility in the wealth distribution than wage/salary workers (Bradford). (Robb 49)

Ethnic Group Backgrounds

At the same time, some ethnic groups are treated more favorably than others because of their nationalities or racial backgrounds. The white majority in the US is the dominant class that controls all US resources. It creates barriers to ethnic advancement based on skin color, financial

73

capital, level of education level, business experience, and human capital. Those practices are employed to determine which group the system will prioritize. Color comes first, capital to start businesses is second, next is educational level, family business experience, and financial capital and human resources. At this point, black people are more marginalized than others when it comes to participating in the giveaway of resources because the system excludes them from everything social, economic, and political.

> The lack of success among black-owned Businesses relative to white-owned Businesses in terms of higher rates of business closure, lower sales and profits, and less employment has been linked to low levels of start-up capital, education, and business human capital and disadvantaged family business backgrounds. (Bates 1997; Fairlie and Robb 2007b). (Robb 4)

Financial Help Denial for Minorities

After the white majority, Asian minority groups are more likely to find the finances they need to start up their enterprises. Financial institutions consider them much like the dominant class in terms of skin color. Most Asians have university degrees, and their human capital is vast in the US. Because of that, financial agencies give them $100,000 to open businesses.

Hispanics who own businesses are generally assumed to be less educated and less white than Asians are. Most of them are Mexicans because their country and the US are neighbors. Hispanic entrepreneurs qualify for $50,000–$75,000 to start up their businesses. Other ethnic groups qualify for at least $50,000 to open businesses, while black entrepreneurs are subject to racial prejudice qualify for only $25,000; the justification for that is that white people and other ethnic groups do not consume the products that black-owned businesses produce. The prediction is that black-owned businesses will not exist for a long time.

> Relatively low levels of human capital may limit the ability of black entrepreneurs to successfully run their

businesses, and restricted access to financial capital may result in undercapitalized businesses and the inability of black firms to "weather" financial storms. (57)

The Profits of the Ethnic Groups

Between 1982 and 2002, the result of minority-owned businesses existed 22,485, 449 firms. White-owned firms 18,320,664, Black-owned firms 1,197988, Latino-owned firms, Asian and Pacific Islander-owned firms 1,137,628. Further, total sales and receipts total $ 8,844,543,267; Whites $ 8, 077, 248, 001, Blacks 92, 681, 562; Latino-owned firms $226, 468,398, and Asian and Pacific Islander owned firms 348,542,296. (53)

There were the properties and profits that white and minority-owned businesses made in the US. It is remarkable that black-owned businesses had been kept at the bottom of the economic sphere.

White and Black Wealth Disparities

There was and still is much inequality and social distance between Whites and Blacks. The disparities between the two groups result from social constructs that exclude black people from all spheres of society, and that is clearly a crime against humanity. In sharp contrast, this sort of genocide is everywhere in the world. Those people are marginalized and stopped from participating in resource redistribution of resources while they pay taxes like other ethnic groups.

Examining the full distribution of wealth reveals even more inequality than revealed by a comparison of medians. Twenty-nine percent of blacks have a net worth that is negative or zero. Forty-five percent of blacks have a net worth of less than $5,000. Only about 11 percent of whites have a net worth that is zero or negative. And less than one-fifth of all whites have net worth below $5,000. At the top of the distribution, only 2.7 percent of blacks have a value of net worth that is at least $250,000. Among whites, 22.2 percent have values of net worth in this range. Comparing asset distributions makes it strikingly clear? Blacks are overwhelmingly more likely to have low asset levels and less likely to have high asset levels than are whites. (Robb 55)

Minority-owned businesses invest in their communities by creating jobs, generating local events, and contributing to the community's safety with police partnerships. Minority-owned businesses are usually in neighborhoods populated by others of the same nationality or ethnicity. These businesses can be corner stores, clinics, markets, restaurants, motels, and gas stations, and they can support social activities in their neighborhoods. Those groups generate funds from their business. They access cash liquidity, mobility, and tax break money.

Black-Owned Businesses' Capital Financial Obstacles

In a sense, black-owned businesses cannot afford to invest in and contribute to their neighborhoods because of the perspective and privilege of Asians, Hispanics, and Whites in terms of gaining financial assistance. Black-owned businesses such as barber shops, beauty shops, motels, corner stores, and restaurants are not frequented that much by Whites and cannot generate money either in tax breaks or from black consumers because a lack of capital reduces their ability to buy goods and services in black neighborhoods.

forms as individual proprietorships, partnerships, or any type of corporation.3 The SBO provides statistics that describe the composition of U.S. businesses by gender, race, and ethnicity. Additional statistics include owners' age, education level, veteran status, and primary function in the business; family-and home-based businesses; types of customers and workers; and sources of financing for expansion, capital improvements, or start-up. Economic policy makers in federal, state, and local governments use the SBO data to understand conditions of business success and failure by comparing census-to-census changes in business performances and by comparing minority-/nonminority- and women-/men-owned businesses. (51)

Micro Financial Data Sources

The author used financial agencies, human rights organization surveys, and federal agencies in much the same way. Those important sources provided reliable information. Furthermore, many scholars put their practical financial analysis experience into making that article available to the academic community and were cited by Robb and Fairlie, including some journals and agencies. To name a few of them are the Current Population Survey, Panel Study of Income Dynamics, Survey of Small Business Finances, Characteristics of Business Owners, the US Census Bureau, and the Internal Revenue Service.

The article inferred that it wanted to make readers aware that in the US, there still existed a significant disparity between multiethnic minority-owned businesses that was linked to racial discrimination and prejudice. This kind of racism is meant to exclude people of color. Gaining access to financial resources to start a business depends on skin color, nationality, education, and financial capital, but black entrepreneurs are the last on the list of minority ethnic groups. That racist attitude caused people to die in poverty and remain homeless, and it destroyed their families.

Such economic discrimination created inequalities between minorities. That practice must stop because the planet has enough resources to redistribute to everyone equally. This article is a message to the financial system to treat minority-owned businesses with the same economic privileges all others receive without discrimination.

The Creation of Patterns of Marginalization

In American society, patterns of marginalization described by Cathy Cohen divide the population into different cleavages associated with various economic statuses. Those statuses give birth to several social classes. From this point, each class has been evaluated as nonidentical.

Essentially Concepted Concepts and Marginalization Analysis

Cohen has four dimensions of marginalization: categorical marginalization, integrative marginalization, advanced marginalization, and secondary marginalization. Connolly points out his four dimensions of essentially contested concepts: oppressive description, openness, internal complexity, and the cluster concept.

The first dimension of marginalization, the oppressive description, links to the first dimension of essentially contested concepts. It refers to categorical marginalization. Categorical margination could be described as Jim Crow laws that dealt with slavery and segregation as legally binding social domination.

The second dimension of marginalization is openness, which shows the historical variance of concepts and the variation in the use of terms to describe ethnic groups such as categorical, integrative, advanced, and secondary marginalization. All those aspects are linked to fate.

Integrative marginalization refers to the civil rights movement that helped marginal groups gain access to some resources and access to public offices by accepting the principles and norms of the dominant class that some observers call the integrative group, the conformists.

The third dimension of marginalization is the advanced class linked to the internal complexity, which is a chronic variation. Variation in the use of the term led to disputes because the integration is partial and selective. The outstanding leader or prominent person has been identified as one who conducts community activities. It has been added to the list and has been integrated. This dichotomy is a subject of an intensive quarrel between other leaders. Nevertheless, the disputes intensified and generated the civil rights movement, which denounced hatred, prejudice, and discrimination. From this viewpoint, the dominant white class gave more opportunities for other social levels to emerge and become successful.

The fourth dimension of marginalization is secondary marginalization; it consists of people who have been successful in the system. Some scholars mention that professionals like singers, basketball players, movie stars, and public officeholders are linked to fate after grabbing a social scale and segregating themselves from other social classes. Some critics say that most of them marry Whites or move to live in white neighborhoods whether in the front streets or back streets. That is the maneuver of American primacy in the local and international political sphere to dominate the economic assets.

The cluster concepts bring the social, economic, cultural, and political issues into focus and find durable solutions to those barriers in the marginal communities that divide society into minority ethnic groups. That phenomenon exists in the world and separates the planet into globes. That could generate other social concepts.

American Primacy

Stephen Walt gives his impression of American primacy. Primacy dominates the global north and the global south countries. The global north constitutes the developed countries while the impoverished global south countries are poor. The US, a superpower, controls almost all spheres and their economies and social, cultural, and political aspects by controlling their access to global resources. The status quo utilitarianism uses a strategy to divide citizens into marginalized groups. In this case, marginalization can take multiple forms including stereotyping, stigmatization, degradation, and assimilation. That happens mostly in the case of African American ethnic groups.

In the same vein that Cathy Choen relates in *The Boundaries of Blackness*, many cleavages of marginalization alleviate different socioeconomic classes. American primacy divides people into various social groups. It has applied an integration policy from the bottom up to find the categorical class. On the top is the secondary marginalization class. In politics, some scholars call it the shadow of the future, which means to wait for your turn. During that period, the power was in control by the primacy leadership because of no civil disobedience. Thus, all protest movements include marches, sit-ins, lawsuits, and violent demonstrations. It has no fear for civil rights leader movements because they are on the waiting list. Most important, on the list are some qualified people in the working class, intellectuals in the middle class, and some privileged members in the marginal communities such as pastors, lawyers, developers, and organizers to whom the officials of the primacy government give some limited access to institutions and resources.

Connolly points out four essentially contested concepts that show how society is divided into different classes for the primacy of well-being and established to exploit human beings' conditions by paying low wages. Marginalization is a form of Jim Crow law that legalizes slavery and segregation. Concepts such as politics, good, and want are managed by the dominant class. White supremacy rules the primacy power locally and internationally, which means the rule of the supremacy class is the same everywhere. Therefore, emerging countries are struggling for basic needs while they are deprived of their natural resources.

Nonetheless, the rich countries deny financial aid to the impoverished countries if they get a chance to get financial assistance from the financial institutions, which could reduce the level of poverty. Most of the time, the interest rate is too high. The dividend must be spent on repaying loans to avoid sanctions. The crucial key of the status quo is to divide people into class categories, and the US reigns over the world by impressing other countries either by soft diplomacy or tough diplomacy.

In comparison, Cohen and Walt share the same concern about socioeconomic dilemmas that the citizens cope with daily such as the violation of their positive and negative rights. In that case, both denounce human rights violations because the hegemonic power does not structurally resolve those issues.

Cohen and Walt address the same phenomenon differently. Cohen used four dimensions of marginalization to discuss the exclusion of people from natural resources and lack of access to public offices.

The essentially contested concept, the marginalization system, could be utilized to put pressure on the dominant class to give some more access to marginal groups. American primacy has to change its socioeconomic approach to the global south countries as a unique superpower pole in the same context.

The Second Question and Its Answer

Emancipation is an act of freeing those held in captivity. Hannah Arendt addressed the situation of German Jews, who were politically emancipated in Germany because their potential wealth played a significant role in German society.

> Jews penetrated into the economy of the state everywhere: in France as farmers of taxes, in Prussia as mint coiners or operators in the state works, in Bavaria as lessees of the royal salt mines, and everywhere as purveyors of military supplies. (Arendt 10)

They showed their preponderance over state affairs and their segregation of people. They exposed themselves to virulent criticism and hatred from the Germans and other ethnic groups. Among other things, Jewish people had the reputation of controlling the political and economic powers where they resided.

> They never once dreamed that they were installed "by the grace of God," but knew very well that they had ascended the throne by the grace of the princes and their own money. (Arendt 7)

At that point, they were accused of coercion and corrupting the government to gain economic access. Further, they owned financial institutions such as banks. German Jews were denounced as prejudiced people and segregated people by other community members. Before World War II, Germany had a lot of respect, prestige, and privilege. It imposed its power, interest, cultural values, and religion on others. As a result, they were politically emancipated in Germany before World War II. Nonetheless, after having enjoyed those privileges, a time of disgrace appeared. The German Jewish community was attacked by an extremist and anti-Semitic regime that committed genocide.

> The history of German Jews, in which the very vanguard of society not only accepted Jews nolens volens, but in

a fit of strange enthusiasm wanted to assimilate them
immediately. (27)

The assimilation saved many Jews over the world and especially
German Jews.

Cohen analyzed the breakdown of black politics in *The Boundaries
of Blackness*. Some scholars argue that the breakdown of black politics is
a political emergence to gain some access to public offices and financial
resources. For a long time, the African American community has been
victimized by stereotypes, degradation, stigmatization, and assimilation
into other ethnic black communities, which excludes black people from
political and economic institutions.

White supremacy generates hatred, prejudice, and discrimination
against minorities. Those attitudes and white supremacy encourage the
masses to stay away from political power, financial institutions, and
national resources. Some scholars reveal that black people are promoted
to other limited privileged classes from categorical, integrative,
advanced, and secondary marginalization socioeconomic classes after
emancipation from the supremacy group. They name the advanced
marginalization group conformists. From this point, they conform to
the dominant class's rules, policies, and norms, for instance, the white
privilege doctrine.

Integrative marginalization alters dominant ideological
practices previously used to justify total exclusion of
marginal group members in order to account for the
limited integration of some oppressed group members.
(Cohen 59–60)

Some scholars call this group the black elite. This group has certain
privileges to access political powers and some institutions. The number
of people is limited, and their opportunities for gaining a heightened
socioeconomic status is also limited. Those selected black leaders who
are accepted and admitted integrate a new paradigm to some limited
access from the dominant class after they are faithful to, make allegiance
to, and obey the norms of the dominant class.

The minorities allow participation after they make their voices heard. While this may be true, African Americans are the rare ethnic group that submits to more prejudice, hatred, humiliation, and discrimination. Black people are stigmatized and misunderstood. Those behaviors are rooted in race and skin color to discriminate against black people. African Americans are discriminated against by negative stereotypes because denigration is a social construction that the dominant class uses to exclude them. They are accused of being HIV/AIDS positive, sexually positive, and recipients of food stamps.

> These narratives further stigmatize and marginalize those members of black communities already on edge, such as young black men, poor single mothers receiving assistance, and unemployed black workers. (Cohen 90)

Equally important, African American communities started to constitute social organizations as a potential resistance force. That consisted of gaining some political positions to include themselves in public offices and get access to resources. They motivated churches and built social clubs that they converted into community developments. That gave them the notoriety they needed to run for local, regional, and national offices. Once they integrated the institutions, they could change the racist policies and extend access to minorities and especially black people.

Financial assistance remained a phenomenon because the criteria still constituted barriers for Blacks to get loans from banks. Even though some democratic institutions are integrated by elected or appointed Blacks, they could do little to enlarge the inclusion because white people were the majority. The inclusion of Blacks in politics was made possible by the civil rights movement, marches, sit-ins, lawsuits, and mass protests. Indeed, some black people were realtors, insurance agents, bankers, store managers, journalists, editors, and public officeholders. They entered the fields of banking, education, and housing provided by the dominant class to some members of the lower classes. The resistance of black people made a strong impact on white supremacy.

The resistance generated by African Americans in response to patterns of exclusion has also been structured around racial unity. Whether with regard to civil rights. (Cohen 91)

In short, it infers the political emancipation of German Jews before World War II and the breakdown of black politics. Both experienced freedom in social, economic, cultural, and political spheres, but the German Jews, after their apotheosis, became victims of genocide. Nowadays, Jews have recovered their previous status. Black people were also emancipated from those social issues. They continue the procedure to keep that emancipation valid and maintain their inclusion in state affairs. In the end, assimilation worked for Jews to save their lives, and civil rights worked for the inclusion of Blacks in politics.

CHAPTER 8

∞

Political Parties

Political parties in the US are the backbones of democracy that bring stability to the institutions that generate social security and the well-being of its citizens. There is a mechanism to implant or transplant democracy into autocratic countries.

Scholars define *democracy* as the freedom of citizens to participate in creating democratic institutions and electing and changing the political personnel at the end of the mandates. The US has political parties' policies to regulate the electoral system including two significant parties—the Democratic Party and the Republican Party—and an electoral college constituted of electors. That constitutes a static election to organize the election on time to renew the elected officials.

It is all to establish the stability of democratic institutions like the three branches of the government—the legislative, judicial, and executive. Dissimilar to that, the implant or transplant of democracy cannot apply to other emerging countries. The application of democracy ignores and works upside down so that hegemonic states have a form of democracy and nonhegemonic states have selective democracy. Haiti had ten years without elected officials at the head of its democratic institutions. At the same time, the United Nations, the European Union, and the US are actively in command in Haiti.

The Importance of Political Parties in Democratic Countries

In some democratic countries, multiple political parties' lack of structure is a threat to democracy; the US's two-party system maintains its democracy. Only the party that monopolizes the politics is authoritarian. One populated party among several nonrepresentatives can maintain democracy, but two major party systems are workable for democracy.

The existence of political parties reveals the presence of a democratic structure in a state, which means that a country chooses a democratic regime based on people's freedom and the protection of human rights.

Political parties in a state that adopts democratic policies open it to political pluralism. At that stage, we ask some questions about democratic policies and conduct a comparative analysis of South Sudan and the United States, two countries in which political parties play a central role.

South Sudan has experienced an antidemocratic regime. Authoritarian and dictatorial regimes automatically reject civil and legal rights. Do political parties contribute to a democratic state and maintain a stable democracy? When can parties gain a permanent position? These questions and a brief story of South Sudan will be explored. In that matter, the responses can confirm or disconfirm the importance of political parties in a democratic system.

Political Parties

Political parties play a tremendous role in building institutions with participation of the people in elections. Democracy is the so-called voice of the people. To that extent, political parties create an internal platform with their mission statements, ideologies, colors, and logos and propose some agendas to the party in the state public affairs programs on local, regional, and national levels. Indeed, the state establishes the regulation policy of political parties and the electoral measures. All parties must follow the same standards if the parties are ranked in the lower, middle, and top level among the voters. The parties can organize the party structure platform from the cities to the national standard from this point. The US has two major political parties—the Democratic Party and the Republican Party. Those parties' responsibilities are to offer expertise to the state to run the country for the benefit of all citizens.

> The party system that is needed must be democratic, responsible and effective, a system that is accountable to the public, respects and expresses differences of opinion, and is able to cope with the great problems of modern government. (ASAP 17)

South Sudan—Brief Story

South Sudan is in North Africa; its capital is Juba. South Sudan detached from North Sudan after social conflicts and civil wars. South Sudan has a good environment including lush savannas and swamplands. It has a rich and biodiverse rainforest. It has many species of wildlife. Its population is estimated to be 13,359,000, and the official language is English. It has no religion, but many people are Christian or Muslim. Forty percent of males and 16 percent of females over age fifteen are literate.

Nineteen percent of its citizens live in urban areas while 80.4 percent live in rural areas. The GNI per capita was $608 in 2016. South Sudan has a bicameral parliament, the National Legislative Assembly, composed of 332, and it has fifty council states. A head of state and government runs the State (Ahmad Alawad Sikainga).

Political Resolutions in South Sudan Conflict

Civil wars in South Sudan have been going on for decades. The last began with a military coup instituted by the head of the army, and more than 2 million people and 4-5 – 5 million killed had to be displaced from local, regional, and even out of South Sudan. The civil wars ended in 1983 via a tripartite political accord between the Sudanese People's Liberation Army, the South Sudan People's Liberation Movement (SPLM), and the government of Sudan, which agreed on the Comprehensive Peace Agreement (CPA) on January 9, 2005.

The CPA initiated a new constitution for South Sudan to determine the rules to run the country (Britannica.com). South Sudan had seven principal political parties; the most prominent was the SPLM, which was involved in negotiations to represent the voice of the civil society beliefs of the people, and it proposed a new agenda for the country. The end of the civil war and the resolution moved the country forward and demonstrated the importance of political parties (Britannica.com).

Political Parties in the US

In the US, the Democratic Party and the Republican Party constitute the leitmotiv of democracy. Their attribution to democracy is significant and supports the US Constitution in terms of the Fourteenth Amendment, which guarantees the positive and negative rights of the citizens.

Political parties engage in democracy by coalition, polarization, and ideology. Most of the time, things do not go well between Democrats and Republicans. Usually, members of Congress compromise on issues so the country can run and so its democracy is stable. Political parties in the US strengthen public institutions and prevent officials from destroying them or changing their policies.

> Political Parties lie at the of American politics. E.E. Schattschneider (1942,1) claimed that "political parties created democracy, and ... democracy is unthinkable save in terms of parties."]" (Aldrich 3)

The Two Major Party Systems

The agendas of the Democrats and Republicans are asymmetric when it comes to social issues that generate competition to attract more members, partisans, and voters. In-group and out-group members discuss the party programs. Those programs will be sanctioned by the voters when they elect officials to implement the agendas. For instance, Republicans opt for tax cuts, a debt ceiling, and small government while Democrats advocate for immigration policies and give the lower class more socioeconomic opportunities.

> Democratic candidates have an incentive to base their campaigns around advocacy of specific domestic policy

programs while encouraging Republican candidates to stress more general rhetorical themes of small government, nationalism, and traditional morality. (Grossmann, Hopkins 11)

Among other things, identity reveals a primary social factor that creates tension in a group of people that engenders the phenomenon of white privilege and marginal groups—the exclusion of minorities from the public offices and public resources. The minorities are accused of taking those public resources out of the dominant class. This fight relies on elections for solutions. The Republican Party works to satisfy the dominant class by giving them more money and opportunities, while the Democratic Party gives everybody the same opportunities regardless of their identity.

There was a powerful idea that my group, in that case, white Americans—was suffering because other "groups," such as immigration or minorities, were getting benefits that they did not deserve. This idea, which was common among Republican voters, also predated Trump. He just leveraged it to his advantage. (Sides, Tesler, and Vavreck 71)

The contribution of political parties helps avoid violence, intrawars, and genocide because a cleansing recuperates and controls all public resources. South Sudan experienced civil war before gaining stability because of the lack of structured political parties like the US, the father and promoter of democracy, has. The significant contributions of Republicans and Democrats make America a dream country.

The Importance of Political Parties in Democratic Countries

The existence of political parties in a democratic country opens the door to politically pluralistic viewpoints. Its institutions can implement national programs and make important decisions to establish the state's authority in different spheres of action including its economy, education, health care, security, communication, and transportation.

The country must establish relations with other countries so they can exchange goods and services including intellectual property. Those spheres of action reveal the domain of the state authorities. However, they cannot decide by political cleavage because it is too dangerous to let a minimal political clan enact anything for a country with 380 million people like the US.

Political parties bring on the floor for discussion their agendas at all stages from the local and national structure of the party, which is a democratic exercise. During elections, political parties present their programs and agendas, and the party considered to have better programs are voted into office. Indeed, those who are elected will keep their electoral promises.

> Even when political parties compete for state power, the competition is built around programs or strategies that would best protect and enhance the achievement of the overarching societal objective. (Awolich 3)

While that may be true, this is the significant role political parties play in a democracy. They involve all people in the same electoral process for effective state programs, which can benefit all political parties.

The Operation of Authoritarian and Dictatorial Regimes

The aristocracy associated with authoritarian and dictatorial regimes automatically rejects civil and legal rights. Those types of government are run by an oligarchy of the wealthiest people, who constitute a fraction of the elite. Certain scholars argue that a branch of multiple elite groups promotes exclusion of the majority to prevent them from accessing the nation's commonwealth. To be effective in that enterprise, they utilize racist words, stereotypes, physical brutality, and genocide. The purpose is to accumulate the resources and distribute them to their relatives, friends, and partisans. That is nepotism. The rest of the people, the majority, thus have no access to public resources and cannot protest.

Such system put in place antidemocratic barriers that force people to be silent, go into exile, go to prison, or die. Political parties are not tolerated in authoritarian and dictatorial regimes.

Political Parties and Their Central Role in a Democratic State

The contribution and attribution of political parties are fundamental; some scholars qualify the political parties as to the motor of the democratic States. Their significant contribution is monitoring a democracy watchdog and maintaining the democratic Aquis that was acquired with blood and discrimination. Such as Civil Rights, Legal Rights, Negative Rights, Positive Rights, and Respect for Human Beings. The potential prevention task that the political parties do in a democratic State raises the respect of the State and imposes the dignity of their citizens as a democratic value.

Value dimension is appropriate for evaluating the issue. Due to the logic of electoral competition, political parties build reputations for defending particular values and for pursuing particular policies; as parties compete over time, such reputations are reinforced. (Petrocik 1996, Sniderman 2000, Sniderman and Bullock 2004, 5)

(Petersen, P.5333-534)

It is marvelous that citizens who are concerned about the future of their countries participate in their development. That is the chief attribute of political parties in democratic nations.

Political Parties Maintain Democracies

The chief goal of political parties is to legitimize their elected officials. The electoral system generates a structured way to organize elections. In democracies, all groups have the right to participate in political debate. Political, social, professional, and religious groups and nonprofits and nongovernmental organizations can offer their perspectives on how to keep a country functioning as a democracy. Constructing a democratic structure requires the participation of people who vote. It is necessary to create a central committee to coordinate such organizational activities.

Then, the elected officials can decide on behalf of the whole organization and nation. That structure is legitimate and legalizes the officials. The officials can implement national agendas to improve opportunities for the citizens.

Who Can Affiliate and Identify the Parties?

Political parties are convincing allies in the electorate and among voters. Most people are affiliated with a party based on its agenda or perhaps based on family traditions. In the end, the party members affiliate and identify themselves based on their political ideology. "Voters and political elites alike were impressed by the changes" (Frymer 1).

Some people refer to themselves as Republicans because they imagine that to be a Republican, they must be white supremacists, Catholics, wealthy, violent, hostile to minorities, and looking for white privileges. Those who identify as Democrats have a positive attitude about democratic values and they respect public institutions, Protestants, the poor, and multiethnics. They are proud to be Americans. They continually advocate for the lower and middle classes, believe in social justice, and defend and support human rights for minorities.

> The Democratic Party guarantees that differences in partisan alignments across all ideological categories will persist among groups defined on the basis of ethnicity, income, gender, and religion. (Grossmann and Hopkins 32)

Variation of Political Parties Position

According to certain scholars, the ideology of a political party can change. However, a party's position can also change at any time over some national issues. The ideology of the Democratic Party switched to the Republican Party and vice versa because politics are always dynamic. For instance, many Republicans are in discord concerning Donald Trump's behavior.

Politicians and political parties have an inherent conflict of interest when implementing political finance reform and, as a result, it is a problematic area in which to enact change. (Lee-Jones 8)

To that extent, parties can have a permanent position. Negotiation, consensus, and compromise are the leitmotiv of political parties that want to promote the rule of democracy.

The Contrast of Political Parties in Democracies

Political parties can differ when it comes to social, economic, cultural, and political issues.

The rhetoric of economic privacy, in contrast, seeks to exclude some issues and interests from public debate by economizing them; the issues in question here are cast as impersonal market imperatives or as "private" ownership prerogatives or as technical problems for managers and planners, all in contradistinction to the public, political matters. (Fraser 19)

The task of a political party that wants to operate in a democracy is delicate because it requires tolerance, patience, wisdom, and the capacity to listen to people. Furthermore, as representatives of a political party designed to work with others, designer groups reflect on proposing a draft to construct or complete and reform policies. Political parties have to cultivate tolerance to conduct meetings depending on the number of people in the audience. Equally important, all those in the audience have the right to express their opinions, ask questions, and wait for answers. If a response is not convincing, people can ask for a clarification.

South Sudan was rescued from civil war by the unique democratic entity trusted as a political negotiator. It is inferred that political parties' existence reveals a democratic structure in a state, which means that a country chooses a democratic regime to protect people's freedom and their human rights.

CHAPTER 9

Human Rights and Individual Freedom

Human rights and individual freedom are guaranteed by the UN's universal declaration and are repeated in the preamble to the US Constitution. Furthermore, the notion of capital punishment is a part of human rights and individual freedom that is protected by the negative right in the US Constitution.

The Management of Human Rights by Governments

The Universal Declaration of Human Rights, called the International Bill of Rights in its preamble, declares that all human beings are created equal and that no one can violate their rights. The government limits the US Bill of Rights to overrule citizens and not what the government should do. Therefore, some concepts will be explored in that writing such as natural rights, the universality of rights, two principal rights, opposing rights, and positive rights.

Those different concepts of human rights carry some connotations that define the legal provision of human rights; likewise, they are efforts to protect people from violating certain rights and provide public goods and services they are entitled to procure as human beings without any excuse. To elucidate the research on UDHR, Australia and the United States were chosen for political comparison concerning human rights.

The Primary Desires of People

All human beings should be guaranteed their primary needs—food, housing, education, employment, and health care among them. Secondary needs include roads, bridges, recreation facilities, sports, communication, transportation, energy, and security. Each of those rights correlates with the other and thus can be interpreted as independent or dependent variables. It depends on the advanced fact. In that case, the primary needs are considered to be independent variables and the secondary desires are considered to be dependent variables that can guarantee consistency of manageable human rights in respect and dignity. The contrast is with the independent variables of human rights. The violation of human rights based on skin color, nationality, gender, race, culture, and religion that are linked to economic, social, cultural, and political issues must be eradicated or improved. Otherwise, human rights will continue to be violated by the entity that has the most power.

Australia and Human Rights

Australia's capital is Canberra, and two significant economic and cultural cities are Sydney and Melbourne. Australia is run by the head of state, Queen Elizabeth II, represented by Governor-General David Hudley. The head of government is Prime Minister Scott Morrison. Its population is estimated at 25,743,000. Its currency exchange rate is $1 = 1.288. Life expectancy for males is 80.4 years and for females is 84.06. The GNI per capita income is US$51,360 (Britannica.com).

Australia is among the countries that signed the treaty, but it is not banned by it. The Age Discrimination Act (1992), the Disability Discrimination Act (1992), the Racial Discrimination Act (1975), the Sex Discrimination Act (1984), and the Australian Human Rights Commission Act (1986) define rights that were inserted into the Australian Constitution. Australia, however, has violated human rights; in 1990, a UNHRC commission found seventeen human rights violations in Australia. The Australian courts cannot hear any complaints about human rights because Australia does not have a bill of rights. According to nwccl.org, there is evidence that the law and practice of human rights in Australia are incompatible, which means that the protection of human rights there needs to be improved.

> This tension is managed through laws and policy, including human rights laws that ensure that our governments act in inappropriate and proportionate ways. (Rigney and Williams 2)

Australia's Positive and Negative Rights

Australia's positive and negative rights seem to be not well provided because the Australian people have certain restrictions on some key human rights. All rights are not fully provided; they include the right to food and freedom of religion.

Australia Positive Rights

The research about Australia's positive rights is a vast independent variable, but it chooses one of the most fundamental rights as a dependent variable to write about, which is food. Food is the first vital element of life; therefore, governments have to furnish people with it in sufficient quantity. There is a debate in Australia concerning food insecurity, food access, food availability, and food use. Those elements determine that the positive rights of the Australian people have been violated. If the one principal need is violated, the other rights such as housing, health care, and education could still be satisfied.

> The paper first considers what constitutes a human rights-based approach to achieving food security. Second, it describes the food insecurity that currently exists among Aboriginal and Torres Strait Islander peoples across the three pillars of food access, food availability, and food use. Third, the paper critically examines recent and current Australian government policy aimed at improving food security. (Deanna)

Australia Negative Rights

The rights negative rights in Australia that it chooses the Religion right to write about negative rights in Australia, which is an independent variable, and the freedom of religion, which is a dependent variable. Religion in Australia is a major controversial social issue. According to some scholars in Australia, there are too many religious sects. Data mention that there are around 6.8 billion people with an average of 70 percent having high restrictions on religion.

> According to the Pew Forum on Religion & Public Life, nearly 70 percent of the world's 6.8 billion people live in countries with high restrictions on religion.4 Religious constraints take two forms: 'official curbs on faith and ... hostility that believers endure at the hands of fellow citizens. In the same way, freedom of religion is in violation as negative as food, which is a positive right violation. (Babie Rochow 1)

Comparing the US and Australia

The US implements the concept of positive and negative in the notion of human rights. In human rights, the US is the champion when it comes to providing positive rights. Moreover, it guarantees the protection of citizens' negative rights. Some states adopt some rights to reinforce but neglect other rights. That is the case in Australia.

What Are Human Rights?

Human rights are norms taken by the UN in a draft proposition that guarantees the respect of human rights. Those sets of dispositions follow the procedure and become a draft, which is submitted to the state governments. The governments send a delegation to participate in the elaborations of documents, called a treaty or international law. The next step is to send the documents to the international personalities for review, ratification, and signing. Once the final draft is signed, it becomes international law for all countries that sign it, and all members must comply with it. Unfortunately, the only superpower country has always excused itself and encourages its allies not to ratify most human rights treaties, for instance, the International Criminal Court.

> Internationally-recognized human rights are commonly understood to encompass those rights to which all persons are entitled without discrimination by the mere fact of being human—that is, rights that cannot be denied or restricted based on culture, tradition, nationality, political orientation, social standing or other factors, but must be protected in fact and given effect by law.

> Broadly speaking, these rights include the most fundamental preconditions for a dignified human existence. They are primarily asserted against government authorities (i.e., must be respected, protected and given effect by the government) but in some instances are also capable of assertion against other individuals in their private capacities (e.g., discrimination). (Steward 2)

Several supranational entities including the US, the EU, and the African Union support the notion of human rights. The US has its own Bill of Rights as does the UN.

National and International Bills of Rights

Both bills of rights reside in people's rights to have their primary and universal needs met. The International Bill of Rights repeals some human rights concepts transplanted from the US Constitution to the UN's Constitution. Jefferson's "All men are created equal" is expanded and clarified as "All human beings are born free and equal in dignity and rights." Our Constitution's Fifteenth Amendment reads, "The right to vote shall not be denied … on account of race, color or previous condition of servitude," and the Nineteenth Amendment reads, "The right of citizens to vote shall not be denied … on account of sex."

> Everyone is entitled to all the rights and freedoms outlined in this Declaration, without distinction of any kind, such as race, color, sex, language, religion, political or other opinions, national or social origin, property, birth, or another status. (Washburne 308)

The US Constitution was created more than 150 years before the UN came into existence. The US Bill of Rights comprised the first ten amendments of the Constitution and was made applicable to the states through the due process clause of the Fourteenth Amendment.

Nature of Rights

Four hundred years later, John Locke spoke of natural rights including the right to hold property and the right to freedom. The natural structure of rights consists in preserving the fundamental rights of all human beings no matter where they are or what country they come from. The most important person is *Homo sapiens*. The nature of rights is universal freedom meaning that all people deserve the same kind of respect and protection regardless of their skin color or social status. Natural rights means that all humans must enjoy the same freedom and the same opportunities.

In contrast to the divine right of kings, people have the right to choose their form of government, and the state was the outcome of a free contract. It had no right to interfere with religious beliefs that are not inconsistent with civil society. However, he did not grant complete tolerance to the atheist because "The taking away of God dissolves all," nor to the Roman Catholic Church in England because of its allegiance to a foreign sovereign." (Washburne 307) Nowadays, there are many theories of human rights without practice to reinforce them. Doubly, some international institutions have contributed to violating those writings on human rights. To illustrate this, Renteln said,

> As is typical in the history of philosophy, what was once a simple notion is often transformed into a much more complicated structure. While this is sometimes useful (and indeed necessary) for certain concepts, it

can obfuscate the essential features of an idea. Rights theories exemplify this tendency to reject more simple accounts in favor of more complex normative structures. (Martin and Nickel 1980, 165)

Some of the so-called simple characterizations of rights, however, do capture the essence of a Right. (Alison Dundes Renteln 2)

CHAPTER 10

The Universality of Human Rights

Respect for human beings must be universal because as *Homo sapiens*, we have the same desires regardless of our color, nationality, or gender. Some conventions and treaties require states to protect the rights of everyone. Louis Henken wrote,

> Debate about the universality of human rights requires the definition of "human rights" and even of "Universality." The idea of human rights is related to, but not equivalent to, justice, good, and democracy. Strictly, the conception is that every individual has legitimate claims upon his or her society for defined freedoms and benefits; an authoritative catalog of rights is outlined in the Universal Declaration of Human Rights. (Henken)

Louis considers human rights to be a democratic value that protects people from all sorts of abuse.

> The rights of the Universal Declaration are politically and legally universal, having been accepted by virtually all states, incorporated into their laws, and translated into international legal obligations. Assuring respect for rights, however, will require the continued development of stable political societies and the commitment to constitutionalism. (Henken)

The states, like international personalities, have the responsibility to create livable environments. The rights and duties of all human beings have to be protected while their negative and positive rights are equally provided.

Variables

There are two types of variables—independent variables and dependent variables. Variances generated by independent variables are dependent variables. Positive and negative rights are considered independent variables. The variances of positive rights are goods and services that the state provides including food, shelter, employment, health care, and security. Negative rights produce variances such as the state's protection of civil and legal rights including freedom of speech, freedom of religion, freedom of association, freedom of press, and freedom to protest against the government.

Positive Rights

Positive rights, considered an independent variable, are the inalienable rights of individuals including the right to life, which was given by God and protected by society and the state. Society has to welcome newborns and educate them on its customs, values, and beliefs. The state must provide them with food and water and medical care so they will be healthy, and it must provide schools to educate them.

The state is also required to provide housing for its people. Childress wrote, "A positive right is a justified claim to someone's assistance" (Childress 2). Governments are in charge of providing goods. The services include but are not limited to parks, schools, hospitals, police protection, road maintenance, electricity, jobs, and commerce.

Negative Rights

Negative rights are independent variables. According to some scholars, negative rights protect us from others' interference with us. Negative rights introduce dependent variables such as life, liberty, the pursuit of happiness, and abortion. Those rights are nonnegotiable; the government cannot deny them. Authorities cannot take life. Authorities do not have the right to take away life or give death to any citizen. In this viewpoint, liberty includes freedom of speech, religion, press, liberty, association, and protest. In that case, women have to decide for themselves whether to have abortions or keep the babies. Childress wrote,

> No party the State, the husband, the parents, or the physician, may interfere with the woman's decision to have an abortion, whatever her reasons; indeed, she is not required to state her reasons to prevent others from interfering with her decision. But the State is not legally bound to fund the abortion, and the physician is not legally bound to perform it, except possibly where certain reasons prevail (such as the protection of the mother's health and Life).

In the end the state has certain limits; it cannot decide in terms of negative rights, but at the same time, it must protect negative rights. Childress said, "A negative right is a justified claim to noninterference" (Childress 2).

Positive and Negative Rights Cause and Effect

The government finances the food, shelter, health care, and so on that it provides for its people; these are basic needs. The government funds these rights with social programs such as food stamps, section H, Medicaid, and Medicare. The primary source of revenue is taxes, which the government redistributes in the form of the services it provides.

Some states cannot afford to provide such services because they fail to collect all the taxes they are due because of fraud and corruption. Some powerful officials keep half or most of the amount they amass. The worst phenomenon is nepotism, where the officials give all opportunities to their relatives, friends, and partisans. In cases like this, the government cannot finance the positive rights of its citizens. The result is a collective revolt or lawsuits against the government.

> Shue grounds his concept of basic rights on a critique of the distinction between negative and positive rights,

and a distinction often appealed to suggest that civil and
political but not economic rights are genuine human
rights. (Hayden 41)

Negative Rights Are in Jeopardy

Negative rights are in jeopardy when the state cannot provide its citizens
with their basic needs. The officials do not monitor the use of public
resources; some money is distributed among partisans or privileged
groups. Then social services cannot be provided by the government.

Governments will restrain the freedom of people by prohibiting
certain negative rights. They can have an antidemocratic reaction to
protesters by arresting and imprisoning them or subjecting them to
genocide. Citizens can overthrow the government, and the officials
can face significant violence. It is the dark side of human rights when
officials cannot be held accountable by the people.

A state might not formally be at war, either externally or
internally, but its social, cultural and legal institutions
may be structured according to discriminatory
beliefs and policies that deny basic rights and access
to education, employment, or health care to certain
individuals. (Hayden 45)

The denial of human beings' rights to education, housing,
employment, religious freedom, and so on are human rights violations
that build up social bombs "even if bombs and bullets are not being
used" (Hayden). Such "unjust social arrangements," as Rawl noted,
"are themselves a kind of extortion, even violence" (Hayden 43). Such
forms of rights exclusion and denial of access to those provoke popular
resistance that leads directly to internal wars.

Negative and positive rights are principal independent variables that
have the legal provision of human rights treaties. Australia's government
fails to provide certain positive rights such as food, and negative rights
fail to guarantee religious freedom. In the US, those rights are fully
applied, and social organizations are watchdogs that keep officials
accountable.

CHAPTER 11

To Possess, to Destroy, and to Repossess

The objective of wars is to possess people's belongings and property and their realms. The poor become poorer and the rich become richer because of this formula of possessing, destroying, and repossessing. This constitutes an imperialist plan to keep north countries distant from south countries, and it creates the fortune of hegemonic leaders. Wars from the Thirty Years' War to the Russian war against Ukraine are the reverse of the new world order. At the same time, democracies can turn into autocracies or anarchies based on hegemonic power and international institutions.

To Possess

Some people gain property by force of arms so they can harvest its natural resources. Human-made disasters can eliminate the structure of life, devastate forests, and make the lives of humans and animals miserable if food production is diminished.

Infrastructures encompass houses, bridges, airports, and hotels that generate independent variables such as police stations, fire stations, restaurants, high-level stores, and multilevel activities that constitute the economy's stability because those activities generate employment.

To Destroy

Sometimes, nonsensical disputes cause unnecessary wars. A lack of good faith can result in tremendous violence that causes the loss of many people. Some treaties, conventions, and accords are in place to prevent such war.

That happened in Iraq, Syria, Ukraine, Haiti, and other countries. Human resources died for no real reason. Property was destroyed, investments went down the drain, and life became expensive; most of the population were living under the poverty line. Some concerned observers argue that the hegemonic power of international organizations considers wars and violence to be fun, killing people to be a game, and destroying properties and people's belongings to be just a distraction. If you dehumanize people, no one will care about them.

To Repossess

Repossession is a game changer; all destruction will be reconsidered, and new investments will be launched to create new leaders, billionaires, and new hegemonic countries.

Haiti is in between two hegemonic states and an international institution. Those three entities are guilty of destroying the country economically, socially, culturally, and politically. Haiti's destruction is so massive that entities cannot find a pivotal solution to repair all the offenses it has been subjected to. France and the United States forced the Haitian government to pay an enormous sum of money for no reason. In 1914, the US seized Haiti's gold reserves that today are valued at $60 billion. The US has refused to remit the gold and institute a mechanism for reparation; it prefers to establish terror regimes to eliminate people who request money to resolve social and economic problems.

The US—The Antipathetic State of Haitians

The US returned some Haitian immigrants to Haiti, who then had to face the political, social, and economic dangers there. The US demonstrates that it cares about the catastrophic situation that put Haiti in the middle to confuse the suffering people. The international community comes with economic, social, and environmental plans, but they are nothing but lies. The international community organized events such as the G7 Summit, the G20 Summit, and the Summit of America to brainwash people who desire a better life.

The Summit of America took place in California in 2022. All countries in North and South America should have been invited, but some countries including Cuba, Venezuela, and Nicaragua did not receive invitations because it was said that they lacked democracy and transparency and were corrupt. If that was the case, why was Haiti invited? The UN violates the Haitian Constitution because it recognizes a president and a prime minister issue from the general election that personage who plays both roles by a tweet from the UN and the US that is illegal. Critics say Haiti defaults from all those situations, which means there is autocracy instead of democracy there. Democracy is thrown away by its founders, which provokes to mass protests, violence, and deep poverty.

The *New York Times* denounced France for its brutal economic act of demanding that Haiti pay it 150 million francs in gold for gaining its independence from France. In 2004, the former president of Haiti, Jean Bertrand Aristide, introduced the demand for the restitution and reparation from France, which caused a coup that sent him to South Africa. According to economic experts, that 150 million francs in gold is valued at $115 billion today.

Why do certain countries cause Haiti so much socioeconomic tribulation? Does Haiti violate any treaties, conventions, or UN resolutions? Does Haiti attack any countries? The international community including the UN, the US, and the Core Group must answer those questions.

Haiti deserves to have reparations from diverse counties for their having impoverished it. Young and old must unite to impose on those countries a demand to furnish money to the Haitians to develop the country. Haitian people must intensify their demands through mass protests, sit-ins, marches, social media, and diplomatic channels to force those countries to restore everything they stole from Haiti.

CONCLUSION

The leaders and international organizations that contribute to the destruction of the world for power, money, and women constantly violate international treaties, conventions, and resolutions.

The world is suffering from all sorts of pathogens and pandemic diseases, political crises, inflation, and economic depression caused by human and natural disasters. Those social calamities occurred due to the mismanagement of world affairs.

This book is presented to scholars, colleagues, critics, observers, family members, and friends. From misery to triumph, I am succeeding. I acknowledge the misery, suffering, and misunderstanding that was the key to abandonment and failure. Dear readers, I am fifty-five and have made it; do not let money, age, or prejudice deviate you from your goal.

Creation of Chicago

Chicago was founded in 1830 by Haitian Jean Baptiste Point-DuSable. Though Chicago is the third-largest city in the US, the presence of Haitians there has not been able to make an influential impact on Chicago.

The first Haitians arrived in 1960 during Duvalier's totalitarian regime; they wanted to flee his dominance. Those immigrants constituted a stable community of workers who were able to sponsor their relatives in Haiti to come to the US, but the old and new generations of Haitians clashed on certain issues; the younger generation thought that the older generation was too conservative and corrupt. The discord occurred because the older generation had not built any infrastructure to orient the new arrivals. But the Haitian American Community Association (HACA) was later created to help new arrivals overcome language barriers and to translate their documents.

Perspective of Politologue Vilio Bacette

Haiti, the first independent black nation, has a remarkable history of battling France's hegemony in an earlier era. That great chapter of human history uncovers the hatred, prejudice, punishment, and plots to exterminate the nation. The loss of Haiti demonstrates the behavior of national and international actors and the dysfunction of international organizations that has led to poverty, starvation, and disease in Haiti.

Repartimiento is a political concept of redistributing national assets, natural resources, and products that other states have seized to the state and people of Haiti.

Creation of the UN

The United Nations was created on October 24, 1945, to promote peace and security globally. The UN's Security Council is dominated by five permanent members (P5) that have veto rights, which they have used to block UN resolutions and treaties.

Multiethnic Minority-Owned Businesses in the US

People immigrate to the US with their dreams of advancing in the economic and educational realms. Asian, Spanish, European, African, Caribbean, and Middle Eastern people come to create better lives for themselves.

The Universality of Human Rights

Respect for human beings must be universal because all people have the same desires regardless of their color, nationality, or gender. Some conventions and treaties protect the rights of everybody without exception.

Positive and Negative Rights—Cause and Effect

Governments fund programs that help get food, water, education, housing, health care, and other necessities of life to those who need them.

To Possess, to Destroy, and to Repossess

Possession, destruction, and repossession are the methods the imperialist north uses to suppress countries in the south. Sadly, humanity is waiting for a savior to liberate it from its oppressors. We must apply and speak the truth and to reverse the old world order based on crime and human rights violations. Haitian people must stand up and revoke some diplomatic relations and deny the ecclesiastical assembly.

REFERENCES

Akee, R., K. Spilde, and J. Taylor. (2015). "The Indian Gaming Regulatory Act and Its Effects on American Indian Economic Development." *Journal of Economic Perspectives* 29(3): 185–208. Retrieved October 15, 2020, from http://www.jstor.org/stable/4355012.

Robb, Alicia M. and Robert W. Fairlie. (2007). "Access to Financial Capital among U.S. Businesses: The Case of African American Firms." *Annals of the American Academy of Political and Social Science* 613 (September 2007): 47–72. https://www.jstor.org/stable/25097948.

Mauldin, M. (2012). "A New Governance Explanation for the Creation of a Minority Economic Development Public-Private Partnership in Florida." *Public Performance & Management Review* 35(4): 679–95. Retrieved September 16, 2020, from http://www.jstor.org/stable/23484761.

Harrell, S. (2001). *The Majority as Minority. In Ways of Being Ethnic in Southwest China*. Seattle: University of Washington Press. Retrieved September 16, 2020, from http://www.jstor.org/stable/j.ctvbtzm1x.18.

McCarthy, K. (2008). "Economic Development in New Orleans." In *An Economic Development Architecture for New Orleans* (15–32). Santa Monica, CA; Arlington, VA; Pittsburgh, PA: RAND Corporation. Retrieved September 16, 2020, from http://www.jstor.org/stable/10.7249/tr547hi.9.

Affigne, T. (2000). "Latino Politics in the United States: An Introduction." *PS: Political Science and Politics* 33(3): 520–27. Retrieved September 16, 2020, from http://www.jstor.org

Arendt, H. (1946). "Privileged Jews." *Jewish Social Studies* 8(1): 3–30. http://www.jstor.org/stable/4615245.

Cohen, J. "The Boundaries of Blackness, AIDS, and the Breakdown of Black Politics."

Connolly, William E. (1983). *The Terms of Political Discourse*, 2nd edition. Princeton, NJ: Princeton University Press.

Awolich, A. (2015). (Rep.). Sudd Institute. Retrieved February 15, 2021, from http://www.jstor.org/stable/resrep11039.

Borz, G. (2017). "Justifying the constitutional regulation of political parties: A framework for analysis." *International Political Science Review/Revue Internationale De Science Politique* 38(1): 99–113. doi:10.2307/26940295.

"Consistency In Public Opinion Formation." *Public Opinion Quarterly* 74(3): 530–50. Retrieved February 24, 2021, from http://www.jstor.org/stable/40927729.

Fraser, N. (1990). "Rethinking the Public Sphere: A Contribution to the Critique of Actually Existing Democracy." *Social Text* (25/26): 56–80. doi:10.2307/466240.

Aldrich, J. *Why Parties? A Second Look.*

Sides, J, Michael Tesler, and Lynn Vavreck. *Identity Crisis The 2016 Presidential Campaign and the Battle for the Meaning of America.*

Kumar, R. (2011). "Political Parties in India and the United States: A Comparative Analysis." *Indian Journal of Political Science* 72(2): 555–66. Retrieved February 15, 2021, from http://www.jstor.org/stable/42761441.

Karlsen, R. and B. Aardal. (2016). "Political values count, but issue ownership decides? How stable and dynamic factors influence party set and vote choice in multiparty systems." *International Political Science Review/Revue Internationale De Science Politique* 37(2): 261–76. Retrieved February 15, 2021, from http://www.jstor.org/stable/44632278.

Childress, J. (1980). "Negative and Positive Rights." *Hastings Center Report* 10(1): 19. doi:10.2307/3560496.

Davy, D. (2016). "Australia's Efforts to Improve Food Security for Aboriginal and Torres Strait Islander Peoples." *Health and Human Rights* 18(2): 209–18. Retrieved April 23, 2021, from http://www.jstor.org/stable/healhumarigh.18.2.

Henkin, L. (1989). "The Universality of the Concept of Human Rights." *American Academy of Political and Social Science Annals* 506, 10–16. Retrieved January 16, 2021, from http://www.jstor.org/stable/1046650.